CITIZEN ADVOCACY WITH OLDER PEOPLE

A CODE OF GOOD PRACTICE

Andrew Dunning

with the Working Party on Citizen Advocacy convened by the Centre for Policy on Ageing and chaired by Lady Lloyd

First published in 1995
by the Centre for Policy on Ageing
25–31 Ironmonger Row
London EC1V 3QP

British Library Cataloguing-in-Publication Data.
A catalogue record for this book is available from
the British Library.

ISBN 0 904139 87 5

Designed and typeset by Eugenie Dodd Typographics.
Printed by Bell and Bain Ltd, Glasgow.

CONTENTS

FOREWORD

by Helen Grew

Having been involved in the Pensioners' Movement for nearly ten years, I am very aware of and concerned about the needs of older people and particularly the special problems facing frail and vulnerable older people.

I am secretary of the West Midlands Pensioners' Convention and a West Midland representative on the National Pensioners' Convention. I am also a member of the Birmingham Social Services Department Inspection Advisory Panel. The need for citizen advocacy has been apparent in the work of each of these bodies. Indeed, I translated this observation into action as a management committee member of Birmingham Citizen Advocacy.

In a period when demographic change is being viewed by governments in a manner close to panic, it is particularly timely that we remember the need to consider the views and interests of the individuals who are part of that change. I am sure that there has always been a need to ensure that the rights of older people are protected. Perhaps in the early part of this century this was mainly provided for by the family. As we look toward the next century, it is apparent that such assistance is no longer readily available.

As someone who has been described as a 'geriatric orphan', I have a personal interest in the creation of a satisfactory network to ensure that when I ultimately require the support of an advocate, it will be there. If I were choosing an advocate for myself I would be torn between peer involvement and that of a much younger person. A contemporary would be more likely to appreciate my problems, but the approach of a different generation with different experiences would be stimulating.

Old age all too frequently produces marginalisation. There is a need to ensure that current emphasis upon community care and bringing services to older people in their own homes does not contribute to this. It must be realised that set against the advantages of remaining at home in a familiar environment are the responsibilities of remaining a householder – paying the bills, claiming benefits, maintaining the fabric of the home. The well-being and quality of life of some older people may only be maintained in such circumstances if they have the support of an advocate.

The alternative of residential care produces its own problems for individuals attempting to exercise their rights and choices. Again, the support of an advocate could be invaluable.

The proposals of all political parties appear to concentrate more and more on self-sufficiency in providing for old age. Targeting benefits and scarce resources for an increasingly ageing population can only mean that some may drop through the net through ignorance of or inability to claim what should be theirs.

I can only see a greater need for citizen advocacy in the future. To identify the need is the easy part. To show how to set up and run a citizen advocacy scheme is where this code of good practice is paramount.

Helen Grew
National Pensioners' Convention

ACKNOWLEDGEMENTS

We are grateful to the many people who contributed towards the production of this Code, at the Consultation Conference in July 1994 and in other contact made throughout the year. Those involved include:

Ken Addis	*Bromley Advocacy Project*
Barbara Avila	*Camden Age Concern Advocacy*
Simon Biggs	*Central Council for Education and Training in Social Work*
David Brandon	*Anglia Polytechnic University*
Fiona Brothers	*Isle of Wight Advocacy Consortium*
Robert Burn	*Newcastle Age Concern Advocacy*
George Carter	*National Pensioners' Convention*
Helen Clarke	*Kingston Citizen Advocacy*
Joan Coker	*Oxfordshire Advocacy Development Group*
Reg Coles	*Wolverhampton Age Concern Advocacy*
Janet Daniels	*Citizen Advocacy in South Glamorgan/ South Wales Advocacy Network*
Rob Donath	*Birmingham Citizen Advocacy*
Gail Elkington	*Carers National Association*
Carole Elliott	*British Association for Service to the Elderly (BASE)*
Helen Grew	*National Pensioners' Convention*

John Harris	*University of Warwick*
Sarah Hayes	*Birmingham Voluntary Services Council*
David Hearnden	*Birmingham Social Services Department*
Iris Holman	*Gloucestershire Age Concern Advocacy*
Lorraine Horton	*People in Partnership*
Jennie Ingram	*Berkshire Alzheimer's Disease Society Advocacy*
Helen Jagielski	*Wolverhampton Age Concern Advocacy*
Adam Jama	*Somali Befriending Project, Liverpool*
Llinos Jehu	*Standing Conference on Citizen Advocacy for Wales*
Jan Killeen	*Alzheimer Scotland – Action on Dementia*
Neil Lambe	*Centre of Medical Law and Ethics, Kings College, London*
Linda Lamont	*Patient's Association*
Jane Lawson	*Hampshire Social Services Department*
Brendon McCormack	*Royal College of Nursing*
Colin McKay	*ENABLE*
Dianne Parr	*Kent Age Concern*
Meena Patel	*Age Concern England*
Bridget Penhale	*British Association of Social Workers*
Pauline Pullin	*SPEAK, Kingstanding*
Marcia Ramsey	*Fife Advocacy Project*
Liz Rickarby	*Cousel and Care*
Joyce Clayton	*Scarborough, Whitby, Filey and Ryedale Advocacy Alliance*
Phil Sealy	*Standing Conference for Ethnic Minority Senior Citizens*
Jef Smith	*Counsel and Care*

Margaret Smith	*Tendring Advocacy*
Members of the Southern Citizen Advocacy Co-ordinators Group	
Les Stannard	*Lewisham Pensioners' Forum*
Cathy Steele	*Wakefield Age Concern Advocacy*
Bob Taylor	*Age Concern Cymru*
Alan Tyne	*Independent teacher and adviser*
Diana Wallace	*Citizen Advocacy in South Glamorgan/ South Wales Advocacy Network*
Henrietta Wallace	*British Medical Association*
Rob Warren	*Citizen Advocacy Alliance*
Rosie Weaver	*Southern Birmingham Community Health Trust*
Liz Whitby	*Tendring Advocacy*
Richard Wood	*Bedfordshire Social Services Department*
Cynthia Wyld	*British Association for Service to the Elderly (BASE)*

INTRODUCTION

'When we talk about needs we mean something more than human survival. We also use the word to describe what a person needs in order to live their full potential. What we need to survive and what we need to flourish are two different things. The aged poor in my street get just enough to survive. The question is whether they get what they need in order to live a human life.' MICHAEL IGNATIEFF (*THE NEEDS OF STRANGERS*, 1990, HOGARTH PRESS, LONDON)

Advocacy is about stating a case, influencing decisions, ending assumptions, getting better services, being treated equally, being included, protecting from abuse, redressing the balance of power, becoming more aware of and exercising rights.

Advocacy can be done by a person or group for themselves or on behalf of someone else. While it has perhaps always existed in a variety of ways, it has recently emerged in particular forms, including that of citizen advocacy.

Citizen advocacy can be defined as a one-to-one ongoing partnership between a trained volunteer citizen advocate and a person who is not in a good position to exercise his or her rights and is at risk of being mistreated or excluded. The citizen advocate should be free from conflicts of interest with those providing services to their partner and should represent the interests of the partner as if they were their own.

The citizen advocacy movement has been growing in Britain since the early 1980s. Initially it focused upon the needs and interests of people with learning disabilities but it has since developed to involve other people who may experience social disadvantage and discrimination, including older people.

The review and consultation report *Speaking Out: Citizen advocacy and older people*, written by Alison Wertheimer and published by the Centre for Policy on Ageing in 1993, set the scene on the scale, status and scope of citizen advocacy projects with older people in Britain. It also highlighted common needs for help in setting up projects, setting standards and surviving as an organisation.

This code of good practice is for the guidance and management of citizen advocacy projects with older people. It is primarily aimed at people involved in setting up and running these projects. However, it will also be of interest to project staff and to partnerships; to service providers who are dealing with advocates and/or considering support to projects; and to the carers, families and friends of older people themselves.

The Code suggests key areas that need to be addressed and highlights the main legal, ethical and practical issues to be considered. Of course, it would be impossible to cover 'all you ever wanted to know about setting up and running a citizen advocacy project but were afraid to ask'. Thus, the reader is referred out of the text to other sources of information and assistance where required.

The Code is not intended to be overly prescriptive. It attempts to codify the elements of good practice – within the project itself and in the relationships between project and advocate, project and partner and advocate and partner – without 'professionalising' an essentially lay relationship. Clearly, projects have to develop good quality advocacy if they are to enable older people who need citizen advocates to attain a good quality of life and obtain good quality services.

The Code is set out in four parts moving from the inspirational issues of 'Getting Started' to dealing with the detail of 'Getting On' with managing the project and creating and supporting partnerships. The final part lists a number of groups and organisations who may offer a range of knowledge and skills or provide mutual support and assistance.

Many people have helped in the production of this Code. A working party was established in November 1993 and ran for one year. It was chaired by Lady (Jane) Lloyd and its members were:

Jane Bearman	Principal Manager, Kingston upon Thames Social Services Department
Phillip Borkett	Operations Director, Methodist Homes for the Aged
Ian Bynoe	Research Fellow, Institute for Public Policy Research (formerly Legal Director, MIND)
Sally Carr	London Development Officer, Citizen Advocacy Information and Training
Navnit Dholokia	Principal Officer, The Commission for Racial Equality
Vera Ivers	Principal Officer (Development), The Beth Johnson Foundation
Claire Johnston	Solicitor, Family Law Team, Law Commission
Carole Newman	Director, Greater London Forum for the Elderly
Jill Pitkeathley	Chief Executive, Carers National Association
Mary Rutherford	Contracts Officer, Age Concern England

For the Centre for Policy on Ageing:

Terri Banks	Project Manager until July 1994 (now Director of the Retirement Income Inquiry)
Gillian Dalley	Director (from October 1994)
Gilly Crosby	Deputy Director
Andrew Dunning	Policy Officer
Marion Peat	Publications Officer

There has been an ongoing process of consultation throughout the year. In July 1994 a two-day seminar was held which brought together people from advocacy projects, pensioners' forums, older people's groups, carers' groups, professional associations and service agencies to consider the first draft of the Code. The valuable contributions made during the seminar were considered along with those gathered from many more individuals, groups and organisations towards this completed version (see 'Acknowledgements', pages 8–10).

It is anticipated that the content of the Code will continue to evolve in line with new developments and changes within the field of advocacy and beyond. Comments and suggestions from users of the Code are welcomed.

Further, whilst the terms of reference for this Code were to produce a code of practice for the guidance and management of citizen advocacy projects with older people, it is recognised that in future it may be possible to go on to produce further sets of guidelines applicable to the needs of other groups who are not the specific focus here.

We are grateful to the Department of Health for funding the completion of this work.

'Citizen advocacy is the sine qua non *of good community care. Linking up a vulnerable individual to a competent member of their community on a one-to-one basis is one of the most effective ways of ensuring not only better services but a better quality of life and a sense of inclusion and belonging within that community.'*

LINDA WARD ('HAVING A SAY IN COMMUNITY CARE'
IN *COMMUNITY CARE*, APRIL 1991)

PART 1

Getting Started

Part 1 outlines the reasons why citizen advocacy can be of benefit to older people and looks at what citizen advocacy is and how it relates to other forms of advocacy. It goes on to pose some of the main questions you will need to consider when you are getting your project started.

1.1 The Need for Citizen Advocacy with Older People

Many older people are well able to represent their own interests in a variety of situations but there are several inter-related issues which may give rise to the need for citizen advocacy:

Population changes

- There has been a large increase in the number of people over 65 in Britain in recent years. Whilst the level of dependency or amount of help needed among older people is often overstated, the chances of becoming confused, frail and disabled increase with age. Thus, more older people are likely to find themselves in a vulnerable position.
- Changes in family structures, living arrangements and patterns of employment mean that some older people might not have a partner or close relative who can provide support or

speak out on their behalf. For others, family relationships are poor and conflicts of interest can arise.

Legislation and policy

- At present, citizen advocacy does not have a legal basis. Sections of the Disabled Persons (Services, Consultation and Representation) Act 1986 which would have given a statutory right to appoint a 'representative' for issues regarding local authority provision of social services have not been implemented. Nevertheless, other legislation and policy does give priority to meeting needs and would suggest the usefulness of advocacy.

- Changes in community care policy and provision since 1990 promote the idea of consumer choice and involvement. Service users are supposed to be at the centre of the new community care structures and processes, from care management to complaints. As around half of all NHS and personal social services users are over 65 this is particularly significant for older people.

- The provision of institutional care in residential care homes and nursing homes is intended to be underpinned by principles of individuality, privacy, dignity, choice and the maintenance of a 'normal' lifestyle. As well as ensuring that an older person is in a position to make everyday decisions, there are times when it is critical to ensure that their views are taken into account, for example when considering the prospect of moving into institutional care, when there is a change in the running of the institution or when it might close.

- The past decade has seen the development of charters and commitments to rights, quality and standards within public services. Nationally, Citizens' Charters currently give the 'consumer citizen' or users of public services a range of entitlements including accessibility, choice, openness, good information, non-discrimination (regarding race and sex – but not age) and redress when required. Locally, a growing number of charters of rights relating to particular services and establishments, such as residential care homes and day centres, have been developed.

Information

- In order to make choices and take action there is a need to have information which is accessible, accurate and understandable. This has become especially important with the emphasis currently being placed upon consumers and clients who can make decisions or choose services having considered the relevant information.
- Finding, interpreting and acting upon information can be difficult. The maze of organisational structures and systems such as local authorities or the Department of Social Security can be hard to negotiate without support. Information might be in a language or format which is difficult to understand or unhelpful.
- Many older people have been described as 'reluctant consumers' who do not or cannot take up available services. There may be a need to offer support in working through information, acknowledging rights and negotiating with officials to obtain entitlements.

Discrimination

- Ageism means that older people may be discriminated against and denied a range of rights because of their age. Social attitudes, policies and services can all help to create and perpetuate negative assumptions and stereotypes. Further, the experience of ageism differs between groups of older people.
- Elders from black and minority ethnic groups face a 'triple jeopardy' – at risk because of their age, the hostile environment in which they have to live and because they do not have access to the services they need. Social policies and services are often based on stereotypes of extended families and communities 'caring for their own'. Provision often ignores particular cultural requirements such as diet, language and religion.

- Around a third of older people are living on incomes at or below the poverty line at Income Support level, and more live on the margins of poverty. Many older people suffer from a poor diet, insufficient heating, lack of household goods and inadequate housing.
- Older people who have been disabled throughout their lives or in later life encounter a 'double discrimination' – being discriminated against on account of their age and their disability. This may result in older disabled people occupying a lower social and economic position.
- Although there are more older women than older men, their life choices and chances can be more limited. Employment history and levels of income in retirement may differ significantly. Assumptions about the roles of men and women can influence service provision as well as support for those who are carers.
- The sexuality of older people is often ignored, ridiculed or treated with hostility. This can particularly be the case for older people who are gay or lesbian. Generally, there is also a lack of attention to sexual health issues for older people, including HIV/AIDS.

Protection

- Older people may be mistreated physically, psychologically, sexually or financially. Such abuse may be at the hands of individuals (including professionals), groups, institutions or organisations who have power over the life of an older person.
- Older people with physical health problems can face substantial change in their lives. Medical treatment options and hospital discharge arrangements can mean making important decisions for the future at a point when the older person is not in a strong position to do so. The wishes of the older person may all too easily be overridden by the assumptions and anxieties of others.

- Older people can be affected by a range of mental health problems which may be longstanding or develop later in life. The onset of dementia brings about a fluctuation and deterioration of a person's ability to make their needs and wishes known and to take decisions. The more distressed or confused a person becomes, the less likely they are to be able to exercise their rights.

- Families and friends who are carers of older people, often older people themselves, can become exploited and exhausted. Although they might not get the services they need to support them in the care they give, they may not make this known for fear of losing what little they do receive.

Participation

- As suggested above, older people should be able to participate in the services they use and to enjoy a full part in wider society. Whilst some older people may feel a sense of belonging within the community, others may be isolated by a range of factors including homelessness, lack of transport or poor social and recreational facilities.

- There has been a steady growth in the membership of organisations which campaign and advance the interests of older people in Britain, for example the National Pensioners' Convention nationally, Midlands Pensioners' Convention regionally and Lewisham Pensioners' Forum locally. Many have expressed the need for advocacy or are themselves undertaking advocacy of various kinds to ensure rights, choices and participation. Some of these organisations are listed in Part 4.

1.2 Types of Advocacy

Older people might need different forms of advocacy at different times, or indeed at the same time in some situations. There are many types of advocacy and as each develops, definitions and distinctions can become blurred. You will need to recognise where citizen advocacy fits into this picture in order to be clear in your purpose. You will also need to be proactive in building alliances with those involved in other forms of advocacy in order to widen choice and participation and to strengthen the advocacy movement as a whole.

Advocacy alongside/on behalf of someone

Citizen advocacy is a one-to-one ongoing partnership between a trained volunteer citizen advocate and a person who is not in a strong position to exercise or defend his or her rights and is at risk of being mistreated or excluded. The citizen advocate should be free from conflicts of interest with those providing services to their partner and should represent the interests of their partner as if they were their own.

Crisis advocacy shares the same principles as citizen advocacy but as its name implies is short term in nature. This tends to be 'one-off' involvement centred upon a particular task or specific situation in which a partner needs the support of an advocate.

Peer advocacy takes place where one person advocates for another who has experienced or is experiencing similar difficulties or discrimination.

Complaints advocacy is narrowly focused upon assisting individuals to pursue complaints within and about particular services, for example a social services department.

Public advocacy refers to the activities of organisations which campaign on behalf of a particular group of people. These are often national bodies with local networks. Some actively seek to involve those they represent in their work, for example Age Concern.

Professional advocacy is perhaps most widely recognised as legal advocacy undertaken by lawyers. However, professional advocacy may also include others who are paid to provide a particular advocacy service, for example welfare and housing rights workers, or professionals who view advocacy as part of their role such as nurses and social workers.

Advocacy by a person/group for themselves

Self advocacy essentially means 'speaking up for yourself'. Self advocacy involves a person who expresses their own needs and concerns and represents their own interests.

Group or collective advocacy in this context means a self advocacy group or organisation which offers mutual support, skill development and a common call for change. This might include a small group of older people who use local services, patients' councils or large bodies such as the National Pensioners' Convention.

1.3 Principles of Citizen Advocacy

You will need to be committed to the essential principles of citizen advocacy:

Independence Avoiding conflict of interest is of paramount concern. It is essential that citizen advocates are independent of agencies or settings which provide services for their partner. They should also be independent of their partner's family or others who might hold separate interests. Similarly, the citizen advocacy office should be independent of service agencies in terms of funding arrangements, administration and setting.

One-to-one relationship The partnership between two individuals is an essential part of citizen advocacy. It ensures that the time and energy of the citizen advocate is focused upon the interests of their partner alone. This differs from professional relationships in which the partner might be one of many clients or consumers. Further, 'partnership' means that there is equality within the relationship where feelings, experiences and growth are shared by the citizen advocate and partner.

Loyalty The primary loyalty of the citizen advocate must be to their partner if they are really to represent his or her interests. This means that loyalty is not placed with those providing services to the partner, families or friends of the partner, or even to the citizen advocacy office itself, but to the partner alone.

Unpaid Unlike others who may enter their partner's life, the citizen advocate is there because they want to be, not because they are paid to be. It is essential that neither the citizen advocate nor their partner see citizen advocacy as a job. Similarly, people should not become citizen advocates to be compensated in some other way, for example using a partnership only as a means of completing community service or getting through a training scheme.

Long-term relationship Citizen advocacy projects should try to develop partnerships on a long-term basis wherever possible. This is because the advocate may need to take time to get to know their partner well before they can really understand their needs and wishes and thus represent their interests in the best way. Many people might also value a longer and perhaps more full relationship. Further, older people with dementia or other progressive illnesses and disabilities may have an increasing need for citizen advocacy as time goes by. However, citizen advocacy projects are not prevented from undertaking crisis advocacy, as described above.

Diversity Citizen advocacy should involve people from a variety of backgrounds and experiences. As many people as possible should have the opportunity of being part of a citizen advocacy relationship or running a citizen advocacy project. This should also mean that people who have been devalued are involved as citizen advocates and project managers, not just as potential partners.

Peer advocacy, where the most suitable advocate for a partner is someone who has experienced similar difficulties or discrimination, can be supported by projects within the principles of citizen advocacy. Alternatively, the partnership might be made up of two people of very different circumstances who choose to share in each other's lives and can make things happen together.

Diversity also means looking in all corners of the community, being proactive in finding people who are 'hidden' as well as those who are more readily identified or who present themselves to the project.

1.4 Citizen Advocacy Roles

Citizen advocacy offices should encourage diversity within the roles undertaken by citizen advocates alongside their partners. Citizen advocate roles may involve giving practical help or emotional support, or both.

Practical help may mean undertaking tasks such as solving problems, taking action and obtaining services. The citizen advocate may be a spokesperson, troubleshooter or information aide. Emotional support may involve meeting a person's needs through compassion, care and concern. The citizen advocate may be a companion, confidante or enabler.

The following stories illustrate practical help and emotional support respectively.

Practical help

Alan is a 65-year-old man who has a learning disability. He has lived with his parents all his life. His father died five years ago and his mother has now died suddenly.

Alan has lived in the same house for 30 years. He is able to carry out most personal care and daily living tasks. He attends a local authority day centre where he is very popular. He is well known to many people in the local area.

Alan's niece has been in touch with the social services department to say that he should be in a residential home as he could not cope for himself in the house. Day centre staff are supportive of this. The day centre is attached to a residential home.

One member of staff at the day centre and a next door neighbour are concerned that Alan does not really want to go into residential care. Instead, he would like to stay in his own home if possible.

Alan was introduced to his advocate Brian. They seemed to get along and were able to discuss Alan's situation and the way in which Brian might help. Brian then undertook to get in touch with those that knew Alan to find out about their involvement and opinions about the future. He found out what services were available to support Alan at home if needed. He attended a case conference alongside Alan to ensure that his views and choices were heard.

The case conference agreed that services could be provided to support Alan at home. Brian checked that everything which was agreed at the case conference was undertaken and kept in regular contact with the care manager responsible for Alan's package of care.

Emotional support

Cleo is an 80-year-old woman who has lived in residential care for ten years. She has not had any contact with family members in that time. Several residents have died in recent years. Many staff have come and gone.

The co-ordinator of the local citizen advocacy project started to visit the residential home on a regular basis and had met with residents and also made a presentation about citizen advocacy to staff. During her visits the co-ordinator had noticed that Cleo was withdrawn and often missed out on activities which other patients were involved in.

Staff said that while Cleo could become distressed she usually 'gives us no trouble at all' and remarked that 'you could forget she was here most of the time'.

The project co-ordinator talked to Cleo about citizen advocacy and she agreed to be introduced to an advocate, Dawn. Over several months Cleo and Dawn's partnership developed. Cleo told Dawn about many of the things that happened in her life and also about her feelings about being 'lonely in a crowd' and 'left behind'. Sometimes Dawn felt that perhaps she wasn't making any difference in Cleo's life, but still wished to continue the relationship.

She later recognised that just 'being there' had made a difference. Cleo was able to be more open, she had started to challenge assumptions that she just wanted to keep herself to herself, staff were taking more time with her and listening to what she wanted rather than deciding for her.

Of course, there may often be some overlap in the roles undertaken by citizen advocates. Once together with their partner the citizen advocate chooses what they feel to be the best ways in which to represent and respond to the interests of that person.

Part 3 of the Code outlines some of the more formal legal roles a citizen advocate might additionally undertake where appropriate.

In understanding what citizen advocacy roles are, you also need to clarify what they are not. Citizen advocacy can become confused with other kinds of relationship, for example mediation, counselling, befriending and advice work, and they may indeed share common skills such as listening, negotiating and being assertive. However, there are clear differences:

Mediation or conciliation services arbitrate or help two parties resolve disputes between themselves; citizen advocates act in the interests of the partner alone.

Counselling includes a wide range of activity and counsellors may be trained in a variety of techniques, from simple problem-solving to those involving psychotherapeutic skills. Citizen advocates aim to develop an equality of relationship with their partner to support them in representing themselves and obtaining their rights.

Befriending involves a volunteer sharing their friendship and social activities with another person; again, the special focus of citizen advocacy is to develop a relationship with regard to rights and representation.

Advice work is usually undertaken by someone who has specific expertise and can give information and make recommendations; citizen advocacy is a wider role in which knowledge is sought and shared together with the partner and where the advocate acts as an aide rather than an advisor.

1.5 Who is it for?

You will need to decide whether your project is aimed at any older person who needs a citizen advocate or is focused upon older people with particular backgrounds, experiences and difficulties. The latter may involve the following considerations:

'Client' groups

Some projects choose to focus their activities on older people who fall within certain service categories or have particular disabilities, such as older people with mental health problems or older people with physical disabilities.

The advantages of doing this are that you can build up expertise, resources and contacts specific to a particular group. Funding might also be dependent upon you working with a particular group.

However, people do not fit into any one readily definable client group, for example an older person might have a physical disability and mental health problems. You will therefore need to build up a knowledge and understanding of a range of issues and concerns with which individuals might be faced.

Specific settings

Some projects concentrate their efforts upon older people in specific settings such as those living in residential care, moving from long-stay hospital into group homes or living alone at home in the community. This approach can have the advantage of dealing with a more 'manageable' number of people and having a more tangible impact within the local area.

However, the decision about which setting to focus upon can be an extremely difficult one – each has its particular problems for older people. Further, these problems are often linked, for example an older person needing a citizen advocate whilst in residential care might have benefited more if that advocate had been introduced while they were still living in the community before the decision to enter residential care was made. Finally, focusing upon a particular setting can lead to the citizen advocacy project becoming too closely associated with a particular service provider or form of provision.

Social groups

Some projects may focus upon the needs of older people in certain groups within society, such as women or people from specific black and minority ethnic groups. This emphasis has the benefit of directly confronting the particular problems faced by these groups, for example sexism and ageism as experienced by women or the 'triple jeopardy' experienced by elders of black and minority ethnic groups (see page 17). Again there is a need to be aware that some people within these groups may need a citizen advocate for a whole range of reasons and therefore a wider understanding is still required.

Legal capacity

Your project might be involved with older people with mental health problems, learning disabilities or dementia, or those who have communication difficulties resulting from concussion, coma or a stroke. In such circumstances you will need to be aware that a person may lack 'capacity' to take his or her own decisions. Here it should be stressed that capacity is a legal concept, not a medical one.

Capacity is not an 'all or nothing' concept. A person may have capacity to take certain decisions but not others. A person might have capacity on some days and not others. Very few people will lack all decision-making capacity.

It was recently said in the High Court for England and Wales that a person has capacity if he or she can understand and retain the information relevant to the decision, can believe that information and can weigh that information in the balance to arrive at a choice. The legal definition in Scotland is broadly the same and the Northern Irish Courts may adopt a similar approach.

Care will be needed in how the project approaches involvement with older people who might lack capacity. This will have a bearing on the selection, training and support offered to the advocates of such partners (see Part 3).

Although advocates do not make decisions on behalf of partners who lack capacity, they may have the time and ability to ascertain and advance the partner's views when others cannot. An advocate who knew the partner before there was any loss of capacity may feel confident enough to say what the partner's views would have been but should not simply state their own views.

Even where it is uncertain what the wishes of the partner are – or indeed whether they have the capacity to consent to the partnership – advocates may still have a role in finding information and standing by the partner when decisions and arrangements are being made.

1.6 What Sort of Advocacy is to be Developed?

When you are setting up a project you will need to be clear from the outset whether you will concentrate purely upon citizen advocacy or attempt to 'mix and match' approaches.

Citizen advocacy alone

Within this model the project workers concentrate upon creating and supporting partnerships. Project workers are discouraged from undertaking advocacy themselves or developing other forms of advocacy within the same project. This is more an issue of practicality than principle – citizen advocacy is time-consuming and difficult to develop. Other activities could distract you from this task.

If you adopt this model it is important that you make strong links with groups and organisations involved in other forms of advocacy. In doing so your project will help ensure that people will get the kind of advocacy they need and that you contribute to the development of the advocacy movement as a whole.

'Citizen advocacy is enough on its own for me! I really have my work cut out here. There are other types of advocacy groups in the area and we keep in contact. It's good to know that we can all put people in touch with whichever group is the most suitable to meet their needs.' June, Project Worker

Multi-approach

Within this model, one or two project staff attempt to develop and support several forms of advocacy, for example a project worker supporting citizen advocacy partnerships, servicing a self advocacy group and undertaking advocacy themselves. This approach recognises that people might need different forms of advocacy at different times or at the same time, and attempts to provide for this under one roof through the same staff.

The main problem with this approach is that it is difficult for relatively few members of staff to sustain everything. In trying to do it all they might spread themselves too thinly and have a limited impact. It might also create the impression that advocacy can be done cheaply and easily and that there is no difference between one sort of advocacy and another.

'I have been trying to juggle citizen advocacy, self advocacy and getting a group together. It seems impossible to please all the people all of the time. In fact, we are putting in bids for another worker so that each of us works on just one side of the project.' MIRIAM, PROJECT CO-ORDINATOR

MULTI-APPROACH/MULTI-SUPPORT

With this model several project staff are employed, each with responsibility to develop and support a particular sort of advocacy, for example a citizen advocacy worker, a self-advocacy development worker, a complaints advocacy worker and so on.

This approach actively recognises the importance of and relationship between different forms of advocacy and that one or all might be required by individuals at different times. For example, an older person with mental health problems might have a citizen advocate but also wish to be part of an advocacy group for mental health service users. This approach may also mean that resources and expertise can be shared with a common purpose. Competition for volunteers and funding might be lessened.

A potential problem with this approach is that the project might become an unwieldy 'empire' to manage. Centralising all advocacy resources in one place might stop the project finding its way into all the corners of the community. Finally, funders might not recognise the need for different parts of the project and might only wish to fund those that deal with large numbers, such as group advocacy, at the expense of others, such as citizen advocacy, which inevitably involve fewer people.

'We've just taken on a complaints advocacy worker to work in parallel with the citizen advocacy worker. We have a lot of knowledge of the area and skills to offer so it seemed to be a good idea to bring this under our umbrella.'

GEOFF, MANAGEMENT COMMITTEE MEMBER

1.7 Who Needs to be Involved?

In establishing your citizen advocacy project you will need to give careful consideration to both the composition of your steering group from which the management committee will develop and to your relationships with service agencies.

The steering group

Membership of your steering group – and eventual management committee – should be made up of local people who have a commitment to citizen advocacy and time to make it work. Ideally, your project will begin as this kind of community response. It may involve:

- older people;
- people with local influence who can form a bridge to politicians, policy makers and funders;
- people who have or are willing to learn useful skills for running the project such as book-keeping and administration;
- people reflecting the diversity and experience of the community, not only as representatives but as contacts who can help forge links with particular groups, for example specific black and minority ethnic groups and people with disabilities;
- once the project is up and running, representative advocates and partners.

There are clear benefits in this model of local people setting up and running their own project:

- it can be stimulating and supportive;
- it can help to develop skills and confidence;
- it can reduce the chance of being taken over or ignored by professionals;
- it can spark off other positive initiatives within the community.

In order for this to work those involved need to:

- develop a clear understanding of advocacy in general and citizen advocacy in particular;
- develop trust and understanding between members;
- listen to each other;
- make sure that the group truly reflects the local community;
- ensure that the group actively encourages and supports new people to get involved.

Service agencies

Service agencies include social services departments and health authorities in England and Wales; social work departments and health boards in Scotland; health and social services boards in Northern Ireland; health trusts and voluntary organisations. Service agencies have become involved in the setting up and running of some citizen advocacy projects. They also fund many citizen advocacy projects in some way. Serious consideration must be given to maintaining citizen advocacy principles in such circumstances.

Service agencies can be positive allies and contributors to your project in a number of ways, including:

- making arrangements which enable citizen advocacy to work effectively, for example agreeing upon access to partners in specific settings and funding procedures;
- formulating policies for their agency and users of their services which include citizen advocacy and related concerns, for example community care plans and residents' rights;
- running training sessions on relevant topics jointly or just for local people involved in citizen advocacy projects, for example community care legislation;
- sponsoring citizen advocacy in attempts to attract funding from local businesses, trusts and other sources, for example providing letters of support;

- dealing with requests from citizen advocacy projects for information and expertise, for example letting them know about the availability of particular services or sharing specialist skills.

You may also be able to protect your principles by being positive and proactive in your relationships with service agencies in the following ways:

Raising awareness
Once you have developed your own understanding of citizen advocacy you will need to spend a significant amount of time promoting an understanding within service agencies at all levels. This might involve one-to-one contact with managers and workers, training and making presentations to groups of staff and circulating relevant literature.

It is essential in order to put the project on the map and to help create the conditions in which citizen advocacy can flourish. It raises awareness of what you are about and your relationship with service agencies and the users of these services. It aids the process of making allies with individuals within the service who will be supportive of the project and know how to relate to it properly. It can enable the project, citizen advocate and service agency to meet the needs of users of the service more sensitively and effectively.

Obtaining funding
If you are seeking or receiving funding for your project from a service agency you will probably be asked to fulfill a contract or service level agreement about your activities in return for the money. You should ensure that the service agency is aware that accountability is not the same as ownership if you are to hold on to your independence.

It is recommended that you should try to tailor your own funding agreement, outlining what the project does and how it can be evaluated both quantitatively and qualitatively.

Quantitative measures need not be based on the number of partnerships alone but upon other indicators, including how many contacts the staff make, how many telephone calls they deal with and how many visits and presentations they carry out.

Qualitative measures may include evidence of adherence to citizen advocacy principles and feedback from people who have been in contact with the project.

You may then need to negotiate with the potential funders to accept this framework of agreement. Many accept that citizen advocacy is not a 'service' in the same way as a day centre or meals on wheels and may be willing to consider contracts which are less rigid in format.

Funding is discussed further in Part 2 (see pages 54–58).

Making decisions
Service agencies who are funders or who have other interests in citizen advocacy may help in the decision-making processes of your project without exercising undue influence over its direction in the following ways:

- by becoming a non-voting member of the steering group or management committee;
- by becoming a member of an advisory group for consultation and support outside the steering group or management committee;
- by undertaking to adhere to citizen advocacy principles within the funding agreement and/or the constitution.

1.8 Where Should it be?

- The citizen advocacy office premises should be independent of those of service agencies. For new projects desperately seeking funding and those surviving on a shoestring, opportunities of low rents and shared resources with service agencies will seem attractive. However, there are substantial disadvantages in such arrangements:

- The citizen advocacy project might at some time find itself placed in a position where there is a clear conflict of interest – does it expose poor practice by a particular service agency when it is using their office space and equipment?
- The citizen advocacy office will become associated with the service agency by local people.
- The citizen advocacy office staff might themselves become more exposed to or confuse their roles with those of service agencies.

Therefore, it is worth spending time looking for a truly independent location for the office. Suitable premises might be found in some community centres, shopping centres, business or enterprise centres.

'We were in a broom cupboard in the hospital. The patients didn't come near us, only the staff.' LESLIE, PROJECT WORKER

- The citizen advocacy office should be located within the geographical area it intends to cover. It should be seen as part of the neighbourhood, not a far-flung outpost.

'It's good being in the middle of things. Right in the middle of the community.' USHA, PROJECT WORKER

- The citizen advocacy project should be an accessible place. Access is important in lots of different ways, but in this context refers only to the physical environment. Within the premises the doors, floors, electrical fittings, toilet facilities and the type and layout of furniture and equipment should all enable access and involvement.

'The whole building is very accessible. Wide doors, raised sockets and so on. We made sure our desks and cabinets were positioned to give everybody the chance to get in and out.'
MIKE, MANAGEMENT COMMITTEE MEMBER

1.9 How will you Communicate?

Communication is central to advocacy. You will need to think early on about communication within your project. This will help to ensure that the project is accessible, sensitive and effective. It will assist the project to present itself in a positive way from the start. You may consider:

Interpersonal skills Members of the steering group or management committee, staff and advocates will need to have the verbal and non-verbal skills required to carry out their roles and tasks.

Communication aids You may need to ensure that your project owns or has access to suitable aids to communication and the training to use them where needed. Such aids to communication may include a minicom, a 'communicator' listening and speaking set and a loop system.

Language itself may need attention in several ways:

- Language should be kept simple and free of jargon wherever possible, for example within project literature, in meetings and in making contacts within the community.
- Access to sign language interpreters or a training in sign language may be necessary to ensure the involvement of people who are deaf.
- Access to interpreting services or the ability to speak particular languages is necessary to communicate with people in the local community whose first language is not English or who would prefer to communicate in another language.

Exchange of stories Many advocacy projects engage in a tradition of storytelling in which issues around partnerships and the project itself are shared, for example within citizen advocacy forums and newsletters. This can be a useful way of spreading ideas about dealing with specific situations, keeping advocacy on a human level and reinforcing its potential.

'We felt that we wanted to be clear on what we are about, break down communication barriers and enjoy the richness of relationships that can result.'

LINCOLN, MANAGEMENT COMMITTEE MEMBER

1.10 Part 1 Further Reading

Beresford, P and Croft, S (1993) *Citizen Involvement: A practical guide for change*. MacMillan, London.

Bernard, M and Glendenning, F (eds) (1990) *Advocacy, Consumerism and the Older Person*. Beth Johnson Foundation, Stoke on Trent.

Brandon, D (1995) *Advocacy: More power to disabled people*. Venture Press, Birmingham.

McEwen, E (ed) (1990) *Age: The unrecognised discrimination*. Age Concern England, London.

Midwinter, E (1992) *Citizenship: From ageism to participation*. Carnegie UK Trust, Dunfermline.

Norman, A (1987) *Aspects of Ageism: A discussion paper*. Centre for Policy on Ageing, London.

Sang, B and O'Brien, J (1984) *Advocacy: The UK and American experiences*. King's Fund, London.

Slater, R and Johnson, J (eds) (1993) *Ageing and Later Life*. Sage, London.

Wertheimer, A (1993) *Speaking Out: Citizen advocacy and older people*. Centre for Policy on Ageing, London.

Willis, E (1988) *Advocacy: Some perspectives for the nineties*. Volunteer Centre UK, Berkhamsted.

Winn, L (ed) (1993) *Power to the People*. King's Fund, London.

PART 2

Getting on: Managing the Project

If you choose to work on a purely informal basis through personal networks alone you may try to get by simply through adhering to the principles and practice of citizen advocacy. However, if you create an organisation which is involved in raising funds, employing staff, recruiting volunteers and maintaining office premises within your community, then you will take on additional legal and management duties. Your project will also need to develop policy for parts of its work.

Many areas of managing a citizen advocacy project are common to managing any voluntary organisation. This Part of the Code outlines the key areas you need to address with reference to citizen advocacy. It also refers to other sources of information for you to follow up. You may obtain guidance on a range of issues from:

- the National Council for Voluntary Organisations;
- the Scottish Council for Voluntary Organisations;
- the Wales Council for Voluntary Action;
- the Northern Ireland Council for Voluntary Action;
- Citizen Advocacy Information and Training (CAIT);
- your local voluntary service council.

The London Voluntary Service Council and the Directory of Social Change produce a range of excellent publications on aspects of the law and good practice in running a voluntary organisation, including those in 'Further Reading' on page 75. The addresses of the above organisations are listed in Part 4.

2.1 Management Committee Roles and Responsibilities

As your project establishes itself as an organisation the initial **steering group** (see pages 31–32) is replaced by the **management committee**. Members will need to take on a range of roles and responsibilities which ultimately enable partnerships to form and be supported on an ongoing basis.

These roles and responsibilities include:

- administering the business of the project, for example adhering to the constitution (2.3) or conditions of charitable status (2.4);
- making, implementing and monitoring policy, for example equal opportunities (2.5), confidentiality and records (2.6);
- dealing with financial matters, for example obtaining funds (2.7) and keeping proper accounts (2.8);
- attending to personnel issues, for example staff recruitment and conditions of service (2.9);
- protecting staff and others involved in the project, for example insurance (2.10) and complaints procedures (2.11);
- advising and supporting project staff, for example providing supervision, training and expertise (2.12);
- making contacts with relevant individuals and organisations, for example potential advocates, partners, service agencies and other advocacy groups (throughout Part 2).

'Being on a management committee isn't just about turning up for meetings in a draughty hall once a month or so. There are important obligations to fulfil. But carrying out your duties means you are helping to make things happen, so that something you care about can flourish.'

GLORIA, MANAGEMENT COMMITTEE MEMBER

2.2 Management Committee Meetings and the Conduct of Business

You may draw up guidelines for the conduct of business in management committee meetings to ensure they function effectively and fairly. In doing so you could consider the following:

Purpose

Management committee members will need to be clear about the purpose of meetings. Meetings may be held for several reasons:

- to carry out your business legally;
- to share information;
- to consult on relevant matters;
- to make decisions affecting the project;
- to provide mutual support toward achieving your goals.

Procedures

Management committee members will need to be clear about the procedures of meetings. This should include an understanding of:

- the use of agenda;
- debating the items;
- quorums;
- making decisions;
- voting processes;
- taking minutes;
- chairing the proceedings.

Participation

Management committee members should be able to participate as fully as possible. This means that you will have to be sensitive towards and overcome common barriers to people taking a full part, including:

- uncertainties about the conduct of business and expectations of roles;
- poor consultation, information or use of time;
- abuse of power or unfair treatment.

You may get over such barriers by:

- establishing a 'pairing' system in which new members are paired with more experienced members to find out more about the workings of the project;
- producing information which is jargon-free and available in a variety of languages and formats, for example tape recordings;
- improving time-management of meetings by putting less on the agenda to enable issues to be discussed fully and at a level understood by all;
- adopting ways of challenging unfair or oppressive assumptions, behaviours and actions;
- undertaking training in areas such as equal opportunities, employment legislation and communication methods.

Some of the work of the management committee may be delegated to **sub-committees** or **working parties**. Such groups enable work to get done between meetings, focus greater attention upon areas of concern and encourage the participation of particular members. The sub-committee or working party may then report back to the management committee.

You may elect **officers** from among the members of the management committee. The main posts are:

- the Chair, who ensures the smooth overall running of the organisation and its meetings;
- the Vice-Chair, who supports the work of the Chair and stands in when needed;
- the Secretary, who undertakes the overall administration of the organisation and its meetings;

- the Treasurer, who deals with financial management issues.

The exact duties of the officers of the management committee will depend upon the strengths and preferences of the individuals involved in your project, decisions of the whole management committee, the roles of staff and what is set out in the rules governing the organisation.

'Some people on our management committee were already used to meetings because of their jobs and so forth. For others it was all new. You have to take everybody with you. Everybody has something to offer, so make sure they all know what's going on and they are involved. It's worth persevering.' CLARA, MANAGEMENT COMMITTEE MEMBER

2.3 The Constitution

A constitution sets out the rules governing an organisation. It is a legal document and *it is strongly recommended that your constitution is drawn up with legal help.*

Among the purposes of a constitution are that it:

- clarifies the aims of the organisation;
- outlines requirements for membership;
- states how decisions are made and disputes are dealt with;
- highlights areas of responsibility and liability;
- gives credibility in dealings with funders, financial institutions and other bodies.

The constitution will include the following:

- name of the project;
- aims and objectives of the project;
- powers of the project to achieve its objects;
- type, terms and timescales of membership;
- size, composition and officers of the management committee;
- quorum of members required to take decisions;
- conduct of elections;

- conduct of management committee meetings;
- conduct of annual general meetings;
- procedures for handling accounts;
- procedures for making changes to the constitution;
- procedures for ending the project.

You may particularly wish to include specific points within relevant sections of your constitution, for example:

- A 'conflict of interest' clause which sets out the position of representatives of service agencies who are funders. This may cover the terms by which they may attend management committee meetings and whether they hold voting rights.
- The involvement of particular sections of the community such as older people and people with disabilities as members of the organisation and management committee.
- That notice of the AGM, minutes of management committee meetings and procedures are made available in a variety of formats (for example audio cassette) and languages to ensure access and involvement of all sections of the community.

The exact form of constitution your project has will depend upon which legal structure it adopts (see below).

'I see our constitution as a practical document – rules for a reason. It puts shape in our management and sets out how we make decisions about our direction.'

VYOMESH, MANAGEMENT COMMITTEE MEMBER

2.4 Legal and Organisational Structure

Your management committee will usually be the governing body of the organisation, with legal, financial and managerial responsibilities. *As citizen advocacy projects may have a variety of origins, you will need to seek guidance from local voluntary service councils and solicitors to work on the specific legal and organisational structure of your project and the responsibilities of its management.* In legal terms, organisations may be unincorporated or incorporated – this section gives a brief account of both.

Unincorporated organisations

An **unincorporated** organisation is a collection of individuals working together without a separate legal existence of its own. This includes unregistered associations, trusts and friendly societies, each with their own advantages and disadvantages:

Unregistered associations
These tend to be small groups with limited and specific purposes and without the intention of employing staff or acquiring property. They may have a set of written rules or constitution.

The advantages of unregistered associations are:

- they may be set up quickly as you do not have to involve other bodies, unless you apply for charitable status;
- they may be set up cheaply since there are no fees to pay, apart from a solicitor's fees if there is a written constitution;
- they are free from interference as they are not accountable to outside authorities;
- they are flexible in that they can more easily make amendments to their purposes or dissolve.

The disadvantages are:

- members of the management committee are 'individually or severally' liable for debts incurred by the organisation;
- property cannot be held in the name of the organisation but by trustees on its behalf;
- legal action and contracts cannot be entered into in the name of the organisation but by members of the management committee as individuals;
- it can be difficult to borrow money in the name of the organisation, so members would have to borrow as individuals.

Trusts

These are usually set up under a will or by the endowment of a gift for a particular purpose. A trust requires a donor, trustees and beneficiaries. It only has a legal identity through the trustees who must ensure that the wishes of the donor are complied with and that they do not benefit themselves. The trust is governed through its Trust Deed or Declaration, which is approved by the Charity Commission for England and Wales or the Inland Revenue for Scotland and Northern Ireland.

The advantages of trusts are:

- they can be quick and cheap to set up and administer;
- amendments are fairly easy to make;
- they are relatively free from interference;
- trustees can hold property and raise funds.

The disadvantages are:

- trusts are neither democratic nor participative, as power rests with the trustees alone;
- if a trustee dies or resigns it can be difficult to transfer to a new trustee;
- trustees are 'individually or severally' responsible if the trust runs into debt, though this might be limited if they have acted in good faith or in accordance with the Trust Deed.

Friendly societies

These are groups with charitable or benevolent purposes. Groups must have a minimum of seven members, a secretary, trustees or officers to take legal action in the name of the society, a registered office and rules acceptable to the Registrar of Friendly Societies.

The advantages of friendly societies are:

- they can take on some of the benefits of charitable status without the involvement of the Charity Commission;
- property can be held and transferred easily;

- there are clear procedures for joining other societies or becoming a company.

The disadvantages are:

- there is some external involvement in the activities of the group by the Registrar of Friendly Societies;
- it does not gain the benefits of having a charity registration number – some funders only give grants to registered charities – unless it also chooses to register voluntarily.

Corporate bodies

A **corporate body** is essentially a body with a separate legal existence from the individuals belonging to it. This includes companies limited by guarantee.

If your project has a substantial income, property and employed staff you might think about acquiring corporate status, usually by becoming a company limited by guarantee. The 'constitution' of a company limited by guarantee is its Memorandum of Association and Articles of Association, which have to be submitted to the appropriate Registrar of Companies for England and Wales, Scotland or Northern Ireland.

The advantages of incorporation as a limited company are:

- members of the management committee may be protected from full personal liability;
- property can be held in the name of the organisation;
- borrowing money can be easier;
- legal action may be taken or defended in the name of the organisation;
- there is a requirement of democratic membership procedures.

The main disadvantages are:

- it can entail more regulation and expense in order to fulfil legal and accounting requirements, for example in drawing up and changing the constitution or submitting annual returns and auditing the accounts.

Charitable status

All of the above organisations may register for charitable status. In order to do so your aims and objectives must meet certain requirements by providing for purposes beneficial to the community. You must also have some form of constitution (see pages 42–43).

It is recommended that projects in England and Wales should contact the Charity Commission for advice and information about registration and conditions. Projects in Northern Ireland should contact the Department of Finance and Personnel for guidance on obtaining charitable status and the Inland Revenue about tax exemptions. Projects in Scotland may also obtain advice from the Inland Revenue.

The main benefits of charitable status are that projects can take advantage of free advice on charity law, tax relief, a range of discounts and greater fundraising opportunities. Indeed, many grant-making bodies have a policy of only assisting an organisation which is registered as a charity.

There are a number of administrative, financial, operational and political conditions imposed upon registered charities. Responsibility for meeting such obligations rests with the trustees of the charity. The trustees will usually be particular members of the management committee of the project who will obviously need to be fully aware of their duties.

Administrative duties include ensuring that the charity runs in accordance with its stated purposes, that responsibility for decision-making is maintained by the trustees and that there are a sufficient number of trustees to work effectively.

Financial duties include ensuring that books of account and consecutive statements of income and expenditure for specific periods are properly kept and submitted as appropriate.

Operational duties include ensuring that the charity treats its beneficiaries fairly and cooperates with other bodies with similar objectives.

There are also **political conditions** which state that charities must not have directly political aims and may only engage in limited political activities.

'I'd say that it is absolutely essential for those involved in management committees to be clear about their responsibilities and potential liabilities within particular structures . . . and whether a structure meets the needs of the project.' GRETA, MANAGEMENT COMMITTEE MEMBER

2.5 Equal Opportunities Policy

You should develop an equal opportunities policy to combat discrimination within your management and employment practices, partnerships and work with the community. There are legal obligations to do so in terms of sex discrimination and race relations legislation. Projects in Northern Ireland will have duties under fair employment legislation with regard to religion and political opinion. There is also a need to confront discrimination on wider grounds such as age, class, disability, illness and sexual orientation. Furthermore, equal opportunities is simply good management practice, fundamental to the effectiveness of any organisation.

It should also be noted that legal duties might be qualified in work with certain groups. For example, if you are running a project aimed only at black elders you would be allowed to recruit only black workers if necessary.

It is important to work at your equal opportunities policy if it is to be fully understood, agreed and owned by your project. It needs to be an active policy which goes beyond being a declaration of good intentions. You may seek further help from relevant publications, courses and organisations such as the Equal Opportunities Commission, the Commission for Racial Equality and in Northern Ireland the Fair Employment Commission.

Your equal opportunities policy may include the following:

Statement of intent

This may include:

- a recognition that discrimination exists;
- the intention of the project to eliminate discrimination in its policies and practices;
- to whom the policy applies;
- a summary of what the project intends to do in order to implement the policy.

The statement of intent may be included in project publications and publicity, recruitment and training packs and on display within the office premises.

The following is an example of an equal opportunities statement of intent from Citizen Advocacy Alliance (CAA), the first project established in Britain. CAA is involved with people with learning disabilities, including older people:

EQUAL OPPORTUNITIES POLICY STATEMENT

Citizen Advocacy Alliance is committed to the principle of equality of opportunity, and is determined to make all efforts to prevent any direct or indirect discrimination or any other unfair treatment of any person on the grounds (for example, but not limited to) of race, nationality, religion, gender, marital status, sexual orientation, age or disability.

This commitment will extend to all activities of CAA, both in its capacity as an employer and also as an organiser of a scheme involving advocates and people with learning disabilities.

Citizen Advocacy Alliance therefore declares that it will introduce measures to prevent any discrimination in its organisation, employment practices and provision of services. These measures will be put into practice through its Management Committee and staff.

Citizen Advocacy Alliance Management Committee and staff will regularly review policy and practice, and ensure that the policy of equal opportunities is being implemented.

Objectives

You should make clear objectives of what you intend to do in order to practice and promote equality of opportunity. These should run throughout all policy and practice of the project.

However, some specific objectives might include the following:

- to make sure that all steering group/management committee members, staff and advocates recognise forms, causes and effects of discrimination;
- to make strong links with groups of people who are discriminated against;
- to make sure that the steering group/management committee reflects the composition of the local community;
- to make sure that the citizen advocacy partnerships reflect the composition of the local community;
- to make sure that the office premises, furniture and equipment enable access and involvement.

Implementation

You should consider how equal opportunities will be put into practice. Among the main points to consider within this process are:

- training of steering group/management committee, staff and advocates;
- staff recruitment and conditions of service;
- finding and making citizen advocacy partnerships;
- examining the structure and activities of the project and identifying where discrimination exists;
- developing procedures for dealing with discrimination within the project.

Making equal opportunities work is the responsibility of everyone concerned with the running of the project. Responsibilities should not be off-loaded onto particular members, for example members of the management committee who are black should not be responsible for issues to do with racism or black elders alone.

Monitoring and review

Projects should beware feeling that they have 'done' equal opportunities or that, by virtue of being concerned with citizen advocacy, their own practice is bound to be 'discrimination-free'. Equal opportunities policies and practices need to be monitored, reviewed and then further developed on an ongoing basis. From the outset it is important to state what the process of monitoring and review will be, how often and by whom.

'Our equal opportunities policy is a central plank of our work – what we are and what we do. It's really important for projects to formulate and operate a strong policy. One which they have really thought about and worked up together.'

Rosemary, Management Committee Member

2.6 Records and Confidentiality

You will have to handle information about individuals which is personal, sensitive and often given in confidence. You will need to be aware of your legal and ethical obligations towards those whose information you have obtained and may hold in records. You could draw up policies and procedures to help you comply with these rules and make them known to all concerned with the project. You will also need to keep records for the purposes of accuracy and fairness.

Your legal duties

These may depend on how the information is held:

- If the information is electronically stored – for example on a computer database – then you will be subject to clear obligations under the Data Protection Act 1984:
  - Those about whom the information relates are, with some exceptions, permitted to have access to the record.
  - The information can only be used for the purposes for which the user is registered and for which it was originally intended.
  - There are strict rules about disclosure of the information, which is generally prohibited. If this applies to you then ensure that you are registered and obtain and read the explanatory material supplied by the Data Protection Registrar (address on page 134).
- If the information is not electronically stored and is recorded in written notes or in a file or is simply within the memory of a member of the project, then the general law of confidentiality will apply. This means that where the project has agreed that the information will be kept in confidence and information has been given as a result, it should not be disclosed at all. You have made what amounts to a contract that binds you to keep it confidential. You can enforce this rule by requiring all employed staff or advocates joining the project to sign a clear declaration that they agree to keep confidential all information which they obtain or receive.

  Even where there has not been a clear agreement of this sort, the law would probably regard the relationship which an advocate or partner has with a project as one where information will have been given in confidence and it will therefore prevent disclosure without the permission of the person concerned. This is because of the nature of the relationship and the nature of the information provided within it. The best rule is to assume that personal information is strictly confidential unless clearly advised of the contrary.

In very rare circumstances there can be a legal justification to disclose confidential information, for example to prevent the risk of an imminent serious crime or the prospect of physical harm to someone, but in the normal course of events this will not apply. It may be important to have a policy statement drawn up with the help of legal advice to show on which defined occasions it may be legally and ethically necessary to breach confidence.

This is a brief confidentiality policy statement from Bromley Advocacy Project, a project involved with people with mental health problems including older people. It is included within a code of practice issued to and signed by the advocate:

The advocacy partnership will be based on the understanding that confidentiality to the partner must be maintained with the exception of:

a The project worker, who in supporting the advocate will be bound by the same confidentiality.

b Serious offences committed by or against the partner or threatened suicide, when both the advocate and the project worker may need to break confidentiality and take further action. The partner will be made aware of these limitations to confidentiality.

Projects may also feel that they wish to disclose certain information about partnerships to others, including:

- funders – who may wish to know more about what they are funding;
- professionals – who may wish to know more about the role of citizen advocacy;
- potential advocates and partners – who may wish to know more about what a partnership might offer;
- management committee members – who may wish to know more about the kinds of issues which arise in practice;
- advocacy workers – who are seeking information or support from others who have experienced similar situations.

Such information must only be disclosed with the consent of the advocate or partner concerned. Even then, the information might be presented without disclosing facts which would identify the individuals concerned. For projects involved with people who lack legal capacity to consent, there are serious ethical considerations before any disclosure.

Finally, you might consider the following in terms of further good practice in recording and office management:

- records should be factual, clear and up to date;
- records should be stored in a safe and secure place;
- records should only be kept for a set period of time;
- advocates should be encouraged to keep a record of financial transactions undertaken on behalf of their partner;
- the project may hold copies of official correspondence, financial transactions or other documentation for safe-keeping if requested and agreed by partnerships.

'Confidentiality and recording isn't just about legal duty. Good practice demands more than the law. There are ethical issues where people may lack capacity to consent to information being disclosed or to understand the implications of disclosure. Be sensitive and be practical. Think carefully about how you use information about individuals in everything you do.' DANNY, MANAGEMENT COMMITTEE MEMBER

2.7 Funding

Given the commitment which is taken on in employing staff and the principle of supporting long-term partnerships, you should develop a fundraising strategy and seek secure and appropriate funding.

The main considerations when seeking funds for a citizen advocacy project include:

- the protection of citizen advocacy principles, and particularly that of independence;

- the availability of funding;
- the adequacy of various types and levels of funding.

When making applications to potential funders you will need to provide a relevant, clear and compelling account of your activities. You will also usually need to show how your work can be evaluated. It is important to stick closely to the priorities and conditions of the potential funder as long as this does not cut across the principles of the project.

You should regularly seek new funding opportunities from a variety of sources. Ideally, this will help to ensure that you do not become overly dependent on one source; that you are prepared when any time-limited funding comes to an end; and that you can move from one funder to another if their conditions become unacceptable.

For most projects obtaining funds is an extremely difficult and time-consuming task. At present there is no statutory or single central source of funding for citizen advocacy though many potential funders, politicians and professionals do support its principles and purposes. Some projects in Britain have endured since the early 1980s and there is growing recognition of their value. It is worth persevering and being proactive in your efforts.

Possible sources of funding include:

- The **Department of Health** has provided funding for a handful of citizen advocacy projects in England and Wales under Section 64 of the Health Service and Public Health Act 1968. This funding is intended for organisations deemed to be in the health or social services field undertaking innovatory work which may be of regional or national significance. It is 'start up' money for a period of up to three years, with a further year for assessment and dissemination.

  Projects in Scotland may approach the **Scottish Office Voluntary Sector Branch** about possible means of funding such as Section 10 of the Social Work (Scotland) Act 1968 and Section 16B of the National Health Service (Scotland) Act 1978.

Projects in Northern Ireland may seek guidance from the **Department of Health and Social Services** or their regional **health and social services board**.

- The **Consortium on Opportunities for Volunteering** sponsors initiatives involving volunteers. It prioritises particular programmes for a maximum of three years. National agents of the consortium include Age Concern England.

  Other appropriate bodies to approach include: for **Scotland**, the Scottish Council for Voluntary Organisations and the Unemployed Voluntary Action Fund; for **Wales**, the Wales Council for Voluntary Action and the Volunteering in Wales Fund; for **Northern Ireland**, the Voluntary Activity Unit at the Department of Health and Social Services; the Northern Ireland Voluntary Development Agency and the Northern Ireland Council for Voluntary Action.

  Addresses of the organisations mentioned above are listed in Section 4.5 (pages 133–138).

- **Local authorities** fund many citizen advocacy projects, usually through social services or social work departments. Before making an application to your local authority you will have to get to know the policies and procedures for funding voluntary organisations. You can get help to find out about these things from your local voluntary services council, relevant officers of the local authority or your local councillor.

  You may find out about mainstream funding for your project or pursue monies for specific purposes, for example if you are involved with older people with mental health problems and/or dementia you may obtain funding through the Mental Illness Specific Grant.

  You may also be proactive in suggesting that the local authority could fund the project through 'top slicing' budgets across departments. This helps to prevent the project being concerned with social services alone and acknowledges partners as full citizens of the authority.

Finally, you will need to be alert to opportunities which may arise for funding out of 'slippage' or underspends within local authority budgets.

If you are successful in obtaining funding the local authority will usually want to enter into a contract or service level agreement with you, as discussed in Section 1.7 (see page 33).

- **Health authorities or boards** can also be approached as potential funders. They will have established policies and procedures which will be in line with purchasing priorities of the particular part of the organisation you deal with, for example hospital trusts or community health trusts.

  As is the case with local authorities you may get help from your local voluntary service council and officers of the authority itself. Again, you will need to work within the principles upon which your project is based in considering a potential contract or service agreement.

- Local authority and health authority **joint funding** arrangements could similarly be explored. These grants may be time-limited or have a 'pick up' commitment by either agency.

- There are a number of national and local **charitable trusts** from which you might obtain a grant. You should check their criteria before making an application. Most trusts will only fund part of the project or only on a time-limited basis. There are several comprehensive directories of trusts which you might find in your local voluntary service council or library, including those listed on page 75.

- Local and large **companies** may also provide support for projects through donations in cash or kind, sponsoring events or publications, and staff secondments. You may approach your local Chamber of Commerce and Trade and your local voluntary service council for suggestions of companies who might support you in your area. You may find useful directories of such companies, including the one mentioned on page 75, through your local voluntary service council or library.

'It is vital to have a fundraising strategy and to make sure that people on the management committee pursue it so that staff are free to do their job – finding and supporting partnerships.' RIVA, MANAGEMENT COMMITTEE MEMBER

2.8 Financial Management

When you have obtained some funding you will need to be aware of the duties, roles and skills involved in financial management. You could make links with people who have accounting and financial management skills and pursue opportunities for further training when available. You may seek further guidance from the organisations listed on page 38 or from community accountancy groups.

KEEPING ACCOUNTS

You must keep accounts for several reasons:

- According to their particular legal structure most projects have a duty in law to keep proper accounts, prepare consecutive statements of account, conduct annual audits of account and make available or hold records of account for a set period.
- Employing staff brings duties to keep records of income tax, National Insurance and statutory sick pay.
- If your project is a registered charity its trustees must ensure that funds are spent in accordance with its constitution or they will become liable.
- Funders require the project to keep records of grant expenditure and check on whether it is being used properly and for the reasons it was intended.

BUDGETS

You should compile a list of budget headings to cover the areas for which funds are required. This will help you to show what you need money for and to monitor how it is being spent. Your list may include:

- salaries;
- employer's National Insurance;
- travel expenses;
- subsistence;
- insurance;
- rent/rates;
- heat/light;
- office furniture;
- office equipment;
- telephone/minicom/answerphone;
- stationery;
- postage;
- publicity;
- training and materials;
- audit/legal/other professional fees;
- other costs and inflation.

It is common practice for a report of running totals to be presented to members at each management committee meeting.

Roles

You may elect a **treasurer** to deal with managing the finances of the project, including budgeting, book-keeping, banking, financial decision-making and preparing for audit. You could also establish a finance sub-committee or sub-group to assist in these tasks.

'A friend of one of the longest-serving members of our management committee was a building society manager. He said that he might be able to spare us some time to help out with money matters. He's turned out to be one of our most enthusiastic members – involved in everything we do, up on all the issues and telling everyone he meets about citizen advocacy!' AMOS, MANAGEMENT COMMITTEE MEMBER

2.9 Personnel Issues

You will need staff to find and train citizen advocates, find partners, match citizen advocates and partners, support partnerships and assist in project administration and development. When taking on workers, you will take on a range of legal duties and management responsibilities. As employers you must be aware of the law and good practice regarding equal opportunity employment. You may be assisted in this process by consulting the sources listed on page 38.

Information on specific areas of employment law and practice can be obtained from the Department of Employment, Department of Social Security, Inland Revenue, Health and Safety Executive, Commission for Racial Equality, Equal Opportunities Commission, Fair Employment Commission (for Northern Ireland), ACAS and Insurance Federations. You may also develop your own contacts in the local community to find people with expertise in personnel matters.

As an employer you will need to deal with staff recruitment and employee terms and conditions of service and pay-related issues.

Staff recruitment

Staff recruitment matters include:

The job description
This should include the job title, the main purpose of the job, to whom the worker is responsible, for whom the worker is responsible, the main duties and hours of work.

The following job description is based on the tasks and responsibilities required of a project worker by Birmingham Citizen Advocacy:

- to find partners;
- to find advocates;
- to train advocates;

- to introduce partners to advocates;
- to provide follow-up and support to partnerships;
- to promote the development of citizen advocacy both locally and nationally;
- to develop and maintain relevant contacts;
- to undergo training as agreed with the management committee;
- to undertake the day-to-day running of the advocacy office;
- to inform partnerships and members of the management committee of training opportunities;
- to keep appropriate records of project activity;
- to present an annual report and other relevant reports as required by the management committee;
- to cooperate with any evaluation as determined by the management committee.

The person specification

This should describe both the essential and desirable skills and qualities needed to do the job. It must be based on the tasks in the job description. Depending upon their organisational structure and priorities, individual projects might differ in what they view as minimum qualifications and experience needed to be eligible.

However, your list might include:

- a commitment to citizen advocacy principles;
- freedom from conflict of interest;
- commitment to equal opportunities and anti-discriminatory practice;
- an understanding of ageism and the problems faced by older people;
- good interpersonal skills with individuals and groups;
- ability to produce reports and accurate recording;
- an ability to set priorities and work alone;
- able to work some evenings and weekends;

- a good knowledge of service provision agencies;
- basic office skills.

The job advertisement
You should seek to advertise as widely as possible within your budget to reach a range of groups. This may include advertising in newspapers, magazines, local radio stations, talking newspapers, job centres and voluntary service council networks. Advertising may be aimed at particular groups including older people, people from black and minority ethnic groups, women and people with disabilities within the relevant media.

The application form
This should be standard and clearly structured. It should only require information relevant for the post and a request for referees should be included. A separate form may be issued for information to monitor equal opportunities in project recruitment, to be completed by applicants voluntarily.

Shortlisting
Members of the management committee should set up a selection panel to be involved in both shortlisting and interviewing. Shortlisting involves making a decision about who to invite for interview based upon whether applications meet the essential and desirable criteria for the job.

Interviews
The selection panel should have preplanned relevant and standard questions to ask each candidate. Each interview should last for the same amount of time and allow for candidates to ask questions of the panel. Candidates should be assessed on the criteria of the person specification. The panel will need to agree upon and be clear about the reasons for their final choice.

'Most projects only have one or two staff, so it is worth spending time on the process of making the right appointment.' KEITH, MANAGEMENT COMMITTEE MEMBER

Terms and conditions of service and pay-related issues

Considerations regarding terms and conditions of service and pay-related issues include the following:

a A contract exists as soon as someone accepts a job offer and this is legally binding on both sides. A written statement of terms and conditions must be issued to employees not later than two months after the start of employment, but in terms of good practice you should provide it as soon as possible.

b The statement of terms and conditions must include the following:

- name of employer;
- name of employee;
- job title;
- starting date;
- hours of work;
- salary scale;
- pay period;
- holiday entitlements;
- sick pay arrangements;
- pension rights;
- disciplinary procedures;
- grievance procedures;
- amount of notice to be given by employer and employee.

It must be stressed that you have an obligation to fulfil these areas. The sources of information and guidance listed on page 60 may help you to do so.

You may also consider including the following additional terms and conditions through good practice:

- flexi-time arrangements;
- religious holidays (in addition to the standard Christian festivals);

- maternity and paternity leave;
- compassionate leave;
- extended leave for visiting relatives abroad;
- leave for caring for relatives and others who are ill;
- travelling and subsistence expenses;
- time off for public duties.

c Contracts for project staff might be fixed-term or open. Projects should consider the nature of their funding, the capacity of the organisation and redundancy provisions in determining the kind of contract to be issued to employees.

Staff support

Working as a citizen advocacy project worker can be a stressful and isolating existence. You will need to offer and provide appropriate support for your staff. This might include regular meetings with a set member of the management committee and developing systems for various members to be available 'on call' if needed urgently.

Supervision may include reviewing the work load, providing a sounding board for difficult issues and making future plans.

Staff should also be provided with training opportunities to develop their values, knowledge and skills base (see Section 2.12).

'There are serious responsibilities in being an employer. Some members of the management committee have been stronger in this area than others. It is good to develop particular expertise in this area and to get access to specialist advice to make sure you are meeting your duties.'

Clarence, Management Committee Member

2.10 Insurance

You will need to obtain appropriate insurance to cover people and property associated with the project. You may contact a local insurance broker to discuss your insurance needs. The British Insurance Brokers Association (address on p 133) could help you find a good firm in your area. Further advice on insurance might also be sought from the organisations listed on page 38.

People

Action or failure to act by an organisation is seen as the responsibility of someone within that organisation. The individual might be a person involved in managing the project, a member of staff or an advocate. Therefore you need to obtain suitable cover for liability that might be incurred in the activities of the project. This may include:

Employer's liability insurance Anybody employing staff has a legal obligation to insure against claims by workers for injury or disease. You must display the insurance certificate in the project office.

Public liability insurance This is also a compulsory insurance. It covers damage, loss or injury caused to any person as a result of negligence on the part of the organisation. This includes any injury to a person visiting the office premises and accidents to those associated with but not employed by the project, for example management committee members.

Professional indemnity insurance This covers claims resulting from incorrect advice. Citizen advocacy projects are not advice bureaux and advocates should be discouraged from giving direct advice to partners. Nevertheless, management committee members, staff or advocates may find themselves in a position where they could be deemed to have given advice. Some projects might extend this insurance to cover defamation as they are involved in representing and writing letters on behalf of people. Professional indemnity insurance is discretionary and costly, so it is worth seeking further guidance about your particular situation.

You might need to clarify the status of advocates, ie whether advocates are deemed by the insurers to be 'employees' or volunteers and whether additional cover or conditions need to be met. Also, you may need to find out whether advocates are covered for certain activities on their own insurance policies, for example vehicle accident insurance, and decide whether the project will meet the difference in any additional premiums.

Property

Premises, contents and equipment may be insured for the market value of the property or the actual cost of replacement. Property insurances include:

Buildings insurance If you are leasing your office, you will need to ascertain whether you or your landlord has the responsibility to take out buildings insurance. If you own your premises there is no legal duty to insure, but it would be difficult to imagine not doing so. You may insure for the cost of rebuilding and the cost of temporary accommodation during rebuilding.

Contents and equipment insurances You may consider various types of insurance covering theft or damage to contents and equipment within the project. Your choice may ultimately be based upon the extent of your property, your activities and costs. You will usually be required to tell insurance companies about the use of the premises and security arrangements. Conditions may be imposed, such as who may use the premises and who may hold keys.

With all types of insurance it is important not to misrepresent or fail to disclose material facts which would affect the level of risk accepted by the insurer within the policy, for example regarding previous claims or changes in the use of the premises. It is also important that insurances are kept up to date and sufficient to cover claims.

'We found big differences in premiums between companies. Some didn't seem to grasp what our situation was at all.

We finally used a company with a special interest in the voluntary sector recommended to us by a similar project to our own.' POLLY, MANAGEMENT COMMITTEE MEMBER

2.11 Complaints Procedures

You should adopt a complaints procedure which is appropriate to your project. The main principles of a complaints procedure are that it should be clear, accessible, prompt, thorough and fair.

There are several possible sources of complaint, for example:

- from a partner about their advocate;
- from an advocate about their partner;
- from relatives or carers of the partner about the advocate;
- from an advocate or partner about the project worker;
- from relatives or carers of the partner about the project worker;
- from service agencies about the advocate, project worker or management.

Each source might have its own possible means of response but ultimate responsibility for complaints procedures rests with the management committee.

Staff grievances are handled through a separate grievance procedure as part of their conditions of employment.

Potential advocates and others should be informed that there is a complaints procedure. They should also be assured that use of the procedure will not lead to victimisation by the organisation.

A judgement might need to be made about the relative seriousness and type of complaint involved, for example whether the issue is a concern or complaint and whether the complaints procedure and/or legal proceedings need to be instigated. An indication of the timescale for the investigation should be given wherever possible.

The following is a complaints procedure used by Scarborough, Whitby, Filey and Ryedale Advocacy Alliance:

Complaints Procedure

Advocacy Alliance tries to provide a quality service. If you are not happy about something we have done you have the right to complain. We hope you feel able to discuss problems with Advocacy Alliance Co-ordinators and Advisory Group/ Management Committee Members at any time. But if you feel you can't do this, or if you have a serious complaint, you should use the complaints procedure. At each stage your complaint will be listened to carefully.

Who can use the complaints procedure?

Anyone can. The procedure is especially for partners, advocates, carers and service providers.

What can you complain about?

You can complain about anything Advocacy Alliance is responsible for, and in accordance with our 'Aims and Objectives'. Advocacy Alliance encourages and supports people involved in advocacy partnerships, whilst recognising that both advocates and partners are free agents independent of the advocacy office.

Advocacy Alliance is responsible for:
the work of Advocacy Co-ordinators; the office; introducing advocates to people who need them; and supporting advocacy partnerships where support is sought.

How do you complain?

You can complain by letter, by phone or by asking to see someone. You can use the attached form, but you don't have to. You are welcome to have someone present your views and help you with your complaint. The person could be a friend, relative, advocate, solicitor or personal representative. If you don't have a representative, the Citizen's Advice Bureau may be able to help.

Who do you complain to?

Your first port of call should preferably be the Co-ordinator, who will try to resolve your problem immediately. If you feel that your complaint has not been resolved to your satisfaction within seven days then the complaint will be written down.

What happens to your written complaint?

You will receive a written acknowledgement that Advocacy Alliance has received your complaint within seven days. Any person or persons named in the complaint will be told that a complaint has been made about them. The complaint will be considered by the Chair of the Advisory Group, one other member and co-ordinator. They will be responsible for asking questions and for making any decisions about how things might be put right. You will be told of their decision, in writing, within 28 days of making your complaint.

What happens if you don't agree with the decision?

An uninvolved co-ordinator will enable you to appeal to a review panel. You should appeal within 28 days of receiving the decision. The panel will consist of the Chair of Advocacy Alliance, a management committee member from another area and another person not connected with Advocacy Alliance. They will investigate your complaint and let you know their decision within 28 days.

This decision will be final.

Advocacy Alliance will make every effort to comply with this decision, but cannot be legally bound by it.

Complaint form

NAME ______________________________

ADDRESS ______________________________

____

____

What do you think Advocacy Alliance has done wrong?

What do you think should be done about it?

Anything else you wish to say?

SIGNED ______________________________

DATE ______________________________

Suitable arrangements for an appeal should be made where the person making a complaint does not agree with the decision following initial investigation.

'At first we were worried about bringing in a complaints procedure – we didn't want to become too bureaucratic with loads of policies and procedures. Then we realised that we would expect service agencies to have one and we had to get our own house in order.'

TOM, MANAGEMENT COMMITTEE MEMBER

2.12 Management Committee and Staff Training

All members of the management committee and staff should have equal access to relevant training. You may develop a training policy for management committee members and staff. This could include considerations of content, process and cost.

Content

You will need to be clear about what you expect from training in terms of values, knowledge and skills. For example:

Values

- citizen advocacy principles and practice;
- equal opportunities legislation, policy and practice.

Knowledge

- social and medical aspects of ageing;
- legal duties and liabilities of organisational management, staff and advocates;
- roles and tasks of management, staff and advocates.

Skills

- specific organisation and management skills, for example time management;
- personal and interpersonal skills and awareness, for example working as a group.

Process

You might consider the following when you are thinking about how to train:

- Induction training should be undertaken with all new management committee members and staff. This might cover the principles and practice of the organisation to enable new members to be effective within it.
- Training might be undertaken on an 'in house' basis by and for yourselves or on an external basis by attending training courses and events and buying in training consultants.
- You may assess the knowledge and skills already held by those involved within your project – a process sometimes called a 'skills audit'. You might then be able to find any gaps and establish what training needs to be sought elsewhere.
- A skills audit can be a good exercise in itself as it helps members to get to know one another and value the

experience each brings to the project. It can also be a sign of members' commitment towards and investment in the future of the project. Partnerships and project staff might be part of this process

- Training should not be viewed as being a 'one-off' event, but as an ongoing process. Management committee members need to keep up with the challenges and changes which affect the project and the partnerships it helps to create and support.
- You may choose to create a training sub-committee on which members are given responsibility for training issues.

Cost

When applying for funding and in using the money you have, you should ensure that you maintain training within your budgets. Holding on to training as a financial priority has practical benefits in the development of the project, its members and its work with partnerships.

'Training is an essential, not an extra. In our management and staff training we've had lots of surprises about what people had done or could do. It can be challenging but great fun too . . . It gives us a common purpose and something to refer back to when particular issues crop up.'

SONIA, MANAGEMENT COMMITTEE MEMBER

2.13 Monitoring and Evaluation

It is important to monitor and evaluate the progress of the policies and work of your project. Monitoring and evaluation can help you to:

- see if you are meeting your objectives;
- identify strengths and weaknesses in your performance;
- make future plans.

As well as being good practice to do so, it might also be a requirement of funders.

Monitoring and evaluation is an ongoing process. You may need to establish how it is going to be carried out in a systematic way. Considerations and ideas include:

- building monitoring and evaluation into all policies and practices – who is going to be responsible and when is it going to be done?
- using time within management committee meetings, sub-committees, etc for monitoring and evaluating specific aspects of policy and practice;
- asking for views and comments about the project from a range of interested individuals, groups and organisations, for example management committee, staff, advocates, partners, local service agencies, people using services and older people's groups;
- inviting a review of your project from a 'peer perspective' by other projects involved in similar work;
- commissioning independent research into your work by interested academics, consultants or policy researchers. This can be costly but may be free as some bodies are keen to build links with the local community and to build up their research profile;
- undertaking a Citizen Advocacy Programme Evaluation (CAPE) study of your project. CAPE was created to review the performance of citizen advocacy projects in the USA. It needs to be adapted to suit the conditions and concerns of citizen advocacy in the UK. Further information about CAPE is available from Citizen Advocacy Information and Training;
- developing appropriate measures of performance with service agencies and funders, as suggested in Section 1.7 (see pages 33–34).

'As well as the usual meetings, we have an "away day" every so often. We choose a nice venue and take a picnic. We go over where we've been – the good, the gaffes and the gaps – and what we're going to do with it all.'

ELAINE, MANAGEMENT COMMITTEE MEMBER

2.14 Contingencies for Closure

Although it might seem a somewhat pessimistic exercise, you should be aware of your responsibilities in the event of having to end the project and make contingency plans for closure. You should seek expert legal and financial advice about facing this task.

You might be facing closure because of debts, loss of a grant or uncertainty about future funding. When such problems arise advice should be sought at the earliest possible stage. Problems rarely dissolve and are usually a lot worse for being left, so get help.

You should find out your exact financial position in terms of assets and liabilities to ascertain how long you can remain solvent. If the project is insolvent without any reasonable chance of reversing the situation it must cease its work.

If you are barely solvent you might plan for survival by reducing costs and/or increasing income. In doing so you will need to take great care not to compromise your principles with regard to any available options or offers of support you receive. Your project should survive only for the purposes for which it was intended, not for a life of its own.

You need to be aware:

- who needs to be informed of the insolvency situation;
- who is liable for the insolvency;
- how to disperse assets;
- how to deal with staff redundancy.

Crucially, you also need to make the best possible alternative arrangements for the support of existing partnerships and individual advocates and partners awaiting a partnership.

'We thought that it was all over when a funder pulled the plug on our main grant aid. We would recommend that any project should make contingency plans before they are in difficulties

– so they are prepared in a calm and considered way, rather than in a state of crisis!'

NICK, MANAGEMENT COMMITTEE MEMBER

2.15 Part 2 Further Reading

Adirondack, S (1992) *Just about Managing: Effective management for voluntary organisations and community groups*. London Voluntary Service Council, London.

Adirondack, S and Taylor, J S (1995) *The Voluntary Sector Legal Handbook*. Directory of Social Change, London.

Age Concern England (1989) *Guidelines for Setting up Advocacy Schemes*. Age Concern England, London.

Casson, D (ed) (1995/96 edition) *A Guide to Company Giving*. Directory of Social Change, London.

Fitzherbert, L *et al* (eds) (1995/96 edition) *A Guide to the Major Trusts*. Directory of Social Change, London.

Forbes, D *et al* (1994 revised edition) *Voluntary but not Amateur: A guide to the law for voluntary organisations and community groups*. London Voluntary Service Council, London.

O'Brien, J and Wolfensberger, W (1977) *CAPE Standards for Citizen Advocacy Programme Evaluation*. NIMR, Toronto.

O'Brien, J (1987) *Learning from Citizen Advocacy Programs*. Georgia Advocacy Office, USA.

Phillips, A (1994) *Charitable Status: A practical handbook*. Directory of Social Change, London.

Read, J (1988) *The Equal Opportunities Handbook*. Interchange Books, London.

Webb, B (1992) *Views from the Inside and Out: The management of the Advocacy Alliance*. Evaluation, Development and Review Unit, Tavistock Centre, London.

Wood, R (1991) *Speak up for Yourself: Putting advocacy into practice*. Age Concern England, London.

PART 3

Getting on: Partnerships

Your project should be aware of and committed to good practice based upon citizen advocacy principles within all its work with partnerships. You will also need to be aware of the legal and ethical duties which derive from the relationships your project establishes and encourages, particularly in regard to the project and the partner, the project and the citizen advocate, and between the citizen advocate and partner.

3.1 Finding Partners

Criteria

Citizen advocacy projects do not have an unlimited supply of advocates. Citizen advocacy project co-ordinators cannot support an unlimited number of partnerships. Yet, many older people in the local community might need an advocate.

In Part 1 it was suggested that you may consider which broad groups of older people your project is to be focused upon, for example older people living in particular settings or older people from particular black and minority ethnic groups. Given that demand for citizen advocacy may always outstrip supply, you may go on to develop more detailed criteria or aids to judgement in finding potential partners.

For example, an older person:

- living alone;
- having little or no contact with family or others;
- frail due to physical health problems;
- receiving or eligible for comprehensive community care support from service agencies;
- being considered for residential care;

or

- living in institutional care;
- having little or no contact with family or others
- living in an institution set to close;
- facing resettlement in the community.

Advertising

Advertising may be carried out by means of:

- local television and radio stations;
- local newspapers and magazines;
- posters and leaflets.

In the use of advertising, you will need to think about audience, content and cost.

Audience

- Community service announcements on local television and radio stations could directly reach a large potential audience. They may also reach a specific group, for example radio programmes broadcast in Asian languages.
- Notices and advertisements placed in newspapers and magazines may similarly have a wide readership and can reach specific groups, for example newspapers aimed at particular black and minority ethnic groups, Braille newspapers and talking newspapers on audio cassette. Some free newspapers which are based on advertising revenue alone may have a limited circulation.

- Posters and leaflets can be a simple but effective way of raising the profile of the project. You will need to think about where to display and distribute them for maximum impact. This might include health centres, residential care homes, community centres and shopping centres. Leaflets are useful because people can keep them for future reference for themselves or someone they know.
- Whichever way you advertise you will need to ensure that the office is ready to receive calls and has good links with other agencies to refer people onto if they seem to need something other than what the project can provide.

Content
In all types of advertising you may ensure that:

- you do not undermine the project or the people it is about through use of ill-considered words or images;
- details of the project are clear and there is no use of jargon;
- you give times when someone will be available to deal with enquiries;
- you state whether there is an answerphone, minicom or other means of communication;
- you state which languages are spoken and arrangements for interpreting where needed;
- you refer to your commitments to equal opportunities and to confidentiality.

Cost

- Advertising on television or radio can be very expensive, as can advertising in newspapers or magazines. However, the local media sometimes provide community service announcements cheaply or free of charge, so it is worth finding out more.
- Instead of advertising directly you may try to obtain the same kind of coverage through feature stories, articles or letters about the project, bearing in mind the above considerations about audience and content.

- Posters and leaflets may be relatively cheap to produce but you will need to consider where they will have greatest impact.
- You may check with potential partners and others who contact the project how they found out about you. This will help you to use your resources in the best way.

Networking

Networking simply means getting to know people in the community and letting them know about the project. This can include individuals, groups and organisations. It can be undertaken in many ways including one-to-one meetings, presentations and training sessions.

- Networking is a core but time-consuming activity, sometimes without immediate results. This needs to be kept in mind when planning and evaluating the activities of the project and its workers.
- When networking you will need to be aware of equality of opportunity. There can be a danger that in using your own existing networks you are only in contact with 'like' people sharing similar backgrounds and experiences. Every effort should be made to tap into a range of individuals and groups in the community other than a restricted few.
- Many citizen advocacy projects report that face-to-face contact is a very effective way of finding partners. This can be particularly important if you are involved with older people with dementia or who are otherwise unlikely to present themselves to the project to request an advocate on the strength of advertising alone. The onus is therefore on the project to get out and about in the community and make yourselves known. The process is much quicker if members of the steering group or management committee also become involved in building networks.

The following sources may provide pathways to potential partners:

Older people
You may try to make contact with individuals and groups of older people in your local area. A range of community groups such as pensioners' forums, pre-retirement associations, carers' groups and tenants' associations include or have links with older people who might need advocates.

The project might directly approach older people using particular health and social services. Project workers might meet up with each individual living in a specific setting such as a hospital ward or residential care home, or make presentations to a large group of residents in the search for partners.

Service agencies
As suggested in Part 1, you will need to raise awareness and obtain the support of service agencies. You will also have to clarify roles and work out arrangements with the service agencies regarding issues such as access and complaints.

Whilst service agencies can be a vital link to potential partners, it is important that they do not decide who will get an advocate – that decision must rest with the project.

Other local people
A range of local people might be informed of what the project is about. You may approach a variety of community organisations, professional and trade associations, clubs and societies. Individuals such as religious leaders, shopkeepers, caretakers and 'beat' police officers may all be aware of people who could need an advocate but do not necessarily receive services or participate in the community.

Consent

When finding potential partners, the issue of consent arises. Many older people will have the capacity to consent to an advocacy partnership if they so wish. Indeed partnerships may rest upon continuing consent and trust between advocate and partner.

Some older people may have capacity at some times and not others, for example those with a mild or moderate degree of dementia. It is up to the advocacy worker to get to know the potential partner and what is 'normal' for them. When is he or she most lucid? What will the potential advocate need to know to begin with?

For older people who lack all decision-making capacity, an ethical judgement is required as to whether to form an advocacy partnership. Again, the project worker may need to spend a great deal of time trying to find ways of communicating, understanding and establishing whether the older person seems happy in the company of someone else on a one-to-one basis. Ultimately, the project worker may judge that it would be preferable to introduce an advocate, due to the particular circumstances being faced by the older person. Here, the concept of 'implied consent' may be introduced.

The project worker may need to undertake more regular, ongoing support of partnerships in which the partner lacks capacity.

'We have found no shortage of potential partners. The challenge has been to reach those who are tucked away in back wards or isolated at home and could be among the most vulnerable. Using contacts in the community and ensuring that they know how to use the project is crucial.'

RORY, ADVOCACY WORKER

3.2 Finding and Selecting Advocates

CRITERIA

You will need to consider carefully who you are looking for to be an advocate. In doing so it can be useful to draw up criteria for potential advocates. For example, she or he should be a person who is:

- free from conflict of interest;
- living in the local area;

- going to live locally for some time;
- linked to useful contacts in the community;
- perceptive and a 'good listener';
- sufficiently assertive;
- able to operate independently;
- honest and trustworthy;
- reliable and loyal;
- resilient and resourceful;
- there for their partner, not other purposes.

You may set yourself the target of ensuring that the advocates you recruit reflect the diversity of people in the local community in terms of age, gender, class, race. Or you might aim at recruiting from a particular group, for example members of a specific minority ethnic group if you determine that to be the focus of the project.

Rather than using your own criteria alone, you should try to find potential advocates who fit the needs and preferences expressed by the partner themselves wherever possible. This is known as **partner specific recruitment** and follows a profile described by the partner rather than the more general criteria put together by the project.

You should be aware that finding advocates takes a great deal of time and effort. To do so you may use the same means as finding partners, through advertising and networking.

Advertising

Use of the media and publicity to recruit advocates is based upon the same general concerns – of audience, content and cost – as efforts to find partners. However, the following are some additional considerations on content:

- You will need to look at the language and images used. Potentially excellent advocates are lost if they cannot understand what citizen advocacy involves.
- It can be useful to highlight people's own experiences or

observations of discrimination or being devalued. You may also draw attention to situations in which they have acted on behalf of or supported someone else. Examples may include accompanying someone to an appointment with their doctor or querying a bill for them.

- You may emphasise the knowledge, skills and experience potential advocates might develop within a partnership.
- You could publicise an 'open' training session on advocacy-related skills such as assertiveness or negotiation. Participants might then be encouraged to go on to become advocates.

Networking

- As is the case in finding potential partners, a wide range of groups and individuals will need to be approached to find advocates. Some contacts might be potential advocates, others may be key people within the community who can suggest where potential advocates could be found. This process is easier if the project workers and steering group or management committee members have firmly established links in the local area.
- Networking may be particularly effective if you are going to undertake partner specific recruitment in finding advocates. This process may begin with project workers checking who is involved with the potential partner – someone already in their life might be an ideal advocate with training and support from the project. However, care needs to be taken to ensure that there would not be any conflict of interest if a person already known to the partner were to become their advocate.
- A large number of approaches to individuals and groups might need to be made before a potential advocate is found for a specific partner. When doing so, project workers may need to bear the following in mind:
    - Confidentiality must be maintained. There is usually no need to give identifying information such as the name of

  the potential partner or exactly where they live – just the circumstances.
  - Balance needs to be achieved in giving the positive strengths and characteristics of the potential partner and not just their problems and difficulties. Similarly, the benefits for the advocate as well as the partner should be stressed.
  - The nature of the practical help or emotional support initially required of the potential advocate should be stated. Possibilities for future development of the partnership may also be discussed if known.
- If you are not successful in finding a potential advocate for a specific partner, those approached will at least have got to know about citizen advocacy and may be able to support the project at a later date.
- If your efforts attract a number of potential advocates, it is advisable to go through selection and training processes with them even if a specific partner has not been identified. The task of project workers is then to find potential partners with whom to match up advocates from the 'pool'. It is important to maintain contact with potential advocates throughout this period to ensure that they do not feel forgotten or unwanted and are not lost by the project.

Advocate recruitment form

You should use an advocate recruitment form as part of your selection process. Such measures are particularly necessary for organisations involved with people who are vulnerable. Project staff may offer to complete the form jointly with a potential advocate as part of getting to know the person. Your form might include the following:

NAME ______________________________

ADDRESS ______________________________

____

____

This might not only be used to contact the potential advocate but also to indicate whether they live near or are accessible to a potential partner.

AGE ____________ GENDER ____________

ETHNICITY ____________ DISABILITY ____________

This information can be used to help match potential advocates with partners if required. It can also be used to monitor equal opportunities and targeting priorities.

PREVIOUS/PRESENT EMPLOYMENT (PAID OR UNPAID):
This might suggest some of the skills and experiences of the potential advocate. It can indicate if there are any possible conflicts of interest due to the nature of the job they do. It may also suggest particular times when they would be able to meet their partner. Again, it can be used to monitor equal opportunities and targeting priorities in terms of employment status and paid or unpaid work.

REASONS FOR WISHING TO BECOME AN ADVOCATE:
This might indicate whether the potential advocate has the kind of attitudes and commitment and experiences which can be harnessed or further developed for an advocacy role.

HOW POTENTIAL ADVOCATES HEARD ABOUT THE PROJECT:
This can help with targeting priorities and use of advertising and networking methods of finding advocates.

REFERENCES:
References provide a further means of getting to know the potential advocate and their suitability for the role. References need not come from professionals or employers, but friends and neighbours in the local community.

Referees should state in which capacity they know the potential advocate. When requesting references, background material on the project, the principles of citizen advocacy and the roles of citizen advocates need to be supplied to the referee.

Criminal records:

You should request a declaration of criminal records from potential advocates. This will provide projects with something of a check on those whose criminal record might preclude them from being advocates. Any convictions for dishonesty, violence, abuse or neglect are of particular relevance here and should be disclosed, given that the nature of the partnership means involvement with a potentially vulnerable older person.

Police checks:

A further part of the selection process which you may wish to consider is the use of police checks. Again, there is a tension between the desire for informality in relationships and concern about the vulnerability of partners.

Police records are confidential and information from them may only be released if it is deemed to be substantially of public interest. Sometimes the information released is partial and you should always be wary of having any false sense of security.

Whilst there is a legal duty on statutory health and social services and some specified voluntary organisations to obtain access to police records for the purposes of child protection and management posts in residential care management (and for the police to provide this information), there is no such requirement regarding older people or other potentially vulnerable adults. As individual Chief Officers of police have discretionary powers to extend disclosure to activities other than child protection, some local advocacy groups may have obtained access, usually through local social services departments, or potential advocates obtaining their own information. The Association of Chief Officers does not encourage such extensions of access and there is already a very heavy demand upon the police records system. Nevertheless, as practice differs between forces projects should find out about the situation in their own area.

As public concern increases about the vulnerability of some older people there may be increasing demands for police checks to be obtained by any organisations involved with such groups. Projects will therefore need to keep up with any shifts in expectation of their responsibilities.

You must never claim that you run police checks if you do not. To do so may make you liable for making false representations or assurances.

'Finding advocates is difficult – they rarely come in droves! It is the most time-consuming part of the work. We use any feasible means of recruitment and check on how people have found their way to us. We still haven't found a set pattern – some have come from the most unlikely sources!'

TAU, ADVOCACY WORKER

3.3 Training Advocates

TRAINING AS SELECTION

A key purpose of training or preparation of citizen advocates is selection. It provides the opportunity to get to know the potential advocate and for the potential advocate to get to know the project. During the training process the suitability of the individual to become an advocate should become apparent through their level of commitment, understanding and interpersonal skills.

The training process may highlight the suitability of the potential advocate to be matched with a particular partner or given situation. It may, for example, emerge that a person is really good at getting people involved in the life of the community or is better at meetings and securing a particular service.

You should also be aware that the drop-out rate can be relatively high in the training of advocates and be prepared for this.

Process of training

- Training can be formal or informal.

  Formal training might involve a time-limited introductory 'course' of structured sessions on set topics. There may also be follow-up sessions on particular issues delivered by project staff or outside presenters or trainers.

  Informal training or orientation might simply entail the discussions held between the project staff and potential advocate. Such discussions might include something of the nature of citizen advocacy, the role of the advocate and the position of the potential partner. Further training would then be delivered on an ad hoc basis in the form of information-giving and support needed to tackle different situations encountered by the partnership.

- Training can be undertaken with individuals or groups of potential advocates.

  Training potential advocates on an individual basis allows issues to be tailored to individual needs and for expectations and concerns to be covered on a more intimate and intensive level. The one-to-one relationship between project staff and potential advocate also echoes that of the partnerships themselves.

  Training groups of potential advocates will save time and enable participants to share their knowledge, skills, expectations and concerns. It may also enhance the feeling of being part of the wider advocacy movement.

- A range of training and orientation methods may be used. These include discussion, presentations, background reading, scenarios, pictures, videos, audio cassettes and site visits.

Content of training

The content of training may vary between and within projects.

Whilst it is not the business of citizen advocacy projects to produce 'experts', you should be able to equip and support advocates to get things done in the interests of their partner. You will need to think about the balance between exploring attitudes and presenting factual information. You may also draw up a set of training outcomes in terms of the values, knowledge and skills you would expect an advocate to hold before being matched with a partner. This might include an understanding of the following:

Values

- ageism and other types of discrimination;
- the experiences of socially valued and devalued groups of people;
- the principles of citizen advocacy;
- equality of opportunity;
- confidentiality
- legal and ethical issues;
- the need for independence in advocacy.

Knowledge

- the rights of older people, for example retirement income entitlements and residents' rights in local authority care;
- aspects of ageing and health, for example dementia or sensory impairments;
- the roles of the citizen advocate, ie practical help and emotional support;
- the responsibilities of the citizen advocate, for example legal roles; non-campaigning within the partnership; avoiding conflicts of interest;
- the structure and organisation of the project, for example members of the management committee and office hours;
- the responsibilities of the project to advocates and partners, for example fulfilling stated commitments to confidentiality and support;
- the range and roles of local service agencies and other relevant organisations, for example the Department of Social Security and citizens advice bureaux.

Skills

- verbal and non-verbal communication;
- assertiveness skills;
- negotiating skills;
- listening skills, for example enabling people to express themselves and checking out what they mean;
- how to use the project and other sources of support and expertise, for example solicitors and community health councils;
- how to undertake 'detective work' in order to find information and ways through various systems, for example local health and social service agencies.

'My training was done in an open and friendly way, but also gave me a firm grasp of the fundamentals before being introduced to Josh, my partner. We covered some core training issues such as principles of citizen advocacy and the roles and responsibilities of everyone to do with the project, but then we also covered gaps in my knowledge and things I wanted to find out before being matched. I liked the informality of the training, but also feel a more competent and effective advocate for Josh, which is paramount.'

MARK, ADVOCATE

3.4 Matching

Matching is a process which begins with the search for potential advocates and partners, particularly when undertaking partner-specific recruitment of advocates. Again, the issue of consent needs careful consideration (see Section 3.1, pages 80–81). The project worker will hold details given by the potential advocates and partners. On the basis of this information the project worker will need to decide whether a partnership might be possible. If so, the following steps may be taken:

- **a** **Individual meetings** with the potential advocate and partner to inform them of a possible match.
- – The worker may give previously agreed details about each to the other.
- – Arrangements for the time and place of the introductory meeting might then be made.
- – The venue for the first meeting needs to be a place where the potential partnership feel at ease and is free from other interests.
- – It is important not to raise expectations about the partnership and to make it clear that it will only go ahead if both wish it to do so.
- – Similarly, your project should never make a guarantee of finding a suitable advocate or partner for a particular individual.
- **b** **Introductory meeting** between advocate and partner.
- – When the potential partnership meets for the first time the project worker may need to help the discussion along to begin with.
- – The worker may then leave the potential partnership alone together for a while during the meeting. This allows them space to see if they might get along without the worker being present.
- – The worker may return later on in the meeting to see if the potential partnership appear to have 'knitted' together.
- – Pressure must not be placed upon the potential partnership to agree to be matched there and then. They should be allowed some time. After the first meeting they should be given space to consider future involvement before making a decision.
- **c** **Further individual meetings** with the potential advocate and partner.
- – The project worker may arrange to meet the advocate and partner individually after they have had time to think about

whether to go ahead with the partnership. More than one such meeting might be required at this stage.

- If the potential advocate or partner choose not to have any future involvement, the project worker may discuss the feelings each of them might have about the decision. This time can be used positively to re-establish the needs and interests of both before trying to make another match for either. In a fragile partnership, it also tends to be better to deal with such circumstances sooner rather than later.

d **Meeting to confirm the partnership** between advocate and partner.

- If both potential advocate and partner decide to form an ongoing partnership the project worker may arrange a further meeting with them together.
- At this meeting the worker may clarify the principles on which the partnership rests and the roles and responsibilities of all parties.

e **Match letters** may be given to the advocate and partner individually. A match letter is a further opportunity to clarify principles, roles and responsibilities. It is also a means of underlining the legal relationships between project and partner, project and advocate and advocate and partner. The 'letter' may take a variety of forms, for example it could be on audio cassette or in Braille.

The following are examples of match letters to an advocate and to a partner:

To the advocate:

Dear Glenys

It was good to meet with you and Connie this week. As you both felt that you would like to be involved with each other, this letter is to confirm your agreement to form a partnership and to highlight again what this means for all concerned.

As Connie described herself, she is very frail physically but clearly wishes to remain in the house where she has lived for 42 years. Several longstanding friends have died in recent years and there are no close relatives. A few of her neighbours and professionals involved in her care feel that she is now in need of some form of institutional care. She is having difficulty in the upkeep of her home and in finding out what might be available to help her to do so.

Although these are the current areas of concern, they might change over the time you are together. As you get to know Connie a little better there may well be other things that you both decide to do.

As Connie's citizen advocate, you will need to keep to citizen advocacy principles. Citizen advocacy is a one-to-one ongoing partnership between a trained citizen advocate who is free from conflict of interest and a partner who needs support to exercise his or her rights and is at risk of being mistreated or excluded. As Connie's advocate, your loyalty is to her alone, and not to any others involved in her life.

You have a duty of confidentiality to Connie which must be maintained, with the exception of:

a The project worker, who in supporting you will be bound by the same confidentiality.

b Situations in which the 'life and limb' of the partner is threatened, when both you and the project worker may need to break confidentiality and take further action.

Connie will be aware of these limits to confidentiality.

You have been told about relevant insurances taken out by the project. You will have also been given a copy of the complaints procedure during your initial training.

Although your partnership is independent of the project, I am here to listen, talk over issues and provide extra back-up and support if required. I may also be able to assist by providing further information and training on specific issues arising within the partnership if needed. If in doubt, ask!

The project may meet reasonable expenses, such as essential travel costs and telephone calls on matters related to the partnership. Such expenses must be agreed to in advance.

There are opportunities for you to take part in the running of the project. Advocate and partner representatives are welcome to attend management committee meetings and relevant sub-groups.

I would be grateful if you could write back to let me know that you have received this letter and agree to the above undertakings.

I wish you well in your partnership with Connie.

Yours sincerely

Karen
Project Worker

To the partner:

Dear Connie

It was good to meet with you and Glenys this week. As you both felt that you would like to be involved with each other, this letter is to confirm your agreement to form a partnership and to again highlight what this means for all concerned.

You described some of the difficulties you are now having in looking after yourself at home and the concerns you have about others wanting you to live in residential care or a nursing home. You want to stay where you are and told me that you would like to find out more about what is available to help you do so.

Although these are your main concerns now, the situation might change over the time you are together with Glenys. As you get to know each other better there may be other things that you both decide to do.

As your citizen advocate, Glenys should keep to citizen advocacy principles. Citizen advocacy is a one-to-one ongoing partnership between a trained citizen advocate who is free from conflicts of interest and a partner who needs support to exercise his or her rights and is at risk of being mistreated or excluded. As your advocate, Glenys's loyalty is to you alone and not to anyone else involved with you.

Glenys has a duty of confidentiality to you which must be kept to, with the exception of:

a The project worker, who in supporting Glenys will be bound by the same confidentiality.

b Situations in which your 'life and limb' is threatened, when both Glenys and the project worker may need to break confidentiality and take further action. Glenys will be aware of these limits to confidentiality.

Although your partnership with Glenys is independent from this project, I am here to listen and provide more information and support on matters arising within the partnership if needed. I have already given you a copy of our project complaints procedure.

The project may meet reasonable expenses, such as essential travel costs and telephone calls on matters related to the partnership. Such expenses must be agreed to in advance.

There are opportunities for you to take part in the running of the project. Advocate and partner representatives are welcome to attend management committee meetings and relevant sub-groups.

I will arrange to come and see you later this week to see if I have made everything clear enough in this letter and that you agree to it all.

I wish you well in your partnership with Glenys.

Yours sincerely

Karen
Project Worker

Projects may also choose to issue a code of practice for citizen advocates to both the advocate and partner as a 'ready reference' to key standards and responsibilities. Copies of this could be given out during initial meetings with the potential advocate and partner.

The following code is based on one used by the Alzheimer's Disease Society Berkshire Branch Advocacy Scheme:

Code of Practice for Advocates

The Advocacy Scheme recruits and supports advocates for people without relatives or with relatives at a distance or abroad, who by reasons of dementia may not be able to articulate, defend or exercise their rights as citizens.

The advocates will:

- attempt to secure their partner's full civil rights as individuals in all areas of living;
- provide long-term practical and emotional support.

This code has been established to secure the rights of people represented by advocates. It recognises the role of any known relatives and people providing services, whilst maintaining the independent status of advocates.

1 The advocate's primary loyalty and commitment is to their partner.

2 An advocacy partnership shall continue as long as both people wish. It can be ended by the advocate or the partner. If the partner is unable to act for him/herself, the partnership may be ended by the Project Worker if necessary.

3 An advocate is entitled to raise any issues which require attention. This includes issues concerning health and social services, employment, housing, transport, access, discrimination, legal matters and financial rights.

4 The advocate shall at all times remember and respect the rights of confidentiality of his/her partner in accordance with the confidentiality policy of the project. An advocate should obtain their partner's consent whenever possible before taking up an issue on their behalf and should not take up an issue contrary to

the wishes of the partner, unless this is within the stated limitations to confidentiality, ie a life and limb situation.

5 The advocate will strive to act in the way their partner would have chosen if he/she had been able to make the choice known. If the partner is unable to communicate his/her wishes clearly, the advocate should seek ways of finding out the partner's preferences and feelings.

6 An advocate should not undertake work normally performed by service providers or others paid to do the task.

7 The advocate should seek the support of the Project Worker if significant difficulties or conflicts of interest arise, so the appropriate information, back-up and support can be given.

8 An advocate will aim to make regular contact where required by their partner.

9 Advocates will ensure equal opportunities for their partners, regardless of class, colour, ethnic origin, gender, religion, sexuality, age or disability.

10 The advocate must be prepared to work within this code which will be reviewed together with the Project Worker after six months.

'We had a gentle introduction. The person from the advocacy [project] took a long time with me on my own and then together with Caroline. She is my advocate now, you know. It's just right. I can tell her anything. I'd given up before this happened – we've moved mountains I'd say.'

WINNIE, ADVOCACY PARTNER

3.5 Frameworks of Support for Partnerships

You may draw up guidelines on follow-up and support which reflect the principles of citizen advocacy, the position of the management committee, the role of project workers and the needs of the partnerships. Considerations include:

Formal and informal support

Advocates may need different kinds of support at different times. This support may be formal or informal. Project workers should be able to assess the kind of support the advocate needs and be able to deliver such support accordingly. They might need to meet the advocate and partner at set intervals on a structured basis to discuss specific developments or any changes in direction taken by the partnership. Alternatively, the project worker might simply follow up partnerships on a more informal basis from time to time to see how things are going.

Frequency

Project workers should be able to assess the amount of support and follow-up to give partnerships and recognise that the frequency may change over time according to the needs of the partnerships. Generally, advocates need more support and follow-up from the project early on in the partnership. Projects can find that it is worth investing relatively more time during this period in order to clarify roles and purposes of the partnership and the project. However, in some situations there might be a constant or increasing need for support, for example if the partner has a dementia or is in a particularly vulnerable situation.

Practical and emotional support

Your project should be able to provide directly for the practical and emotional support needs of advocates. The project worker may act as a sounding board for ideas and ways of dealing with particular issues; provide practical help through the use of office equipment, stationery and other resources; and give information and emotional support to the advocate. Training should also be made available on a continuing basis to meet the specific needs of partnerships

Your project should also be able to assist advocates indirectly by providing access to useful contacts such as consultant geriatricians, solicitors and welfare rights advisers. These professional 'allies' or advocate associates should be sought through the networking process for their specific knowledge and skills. They could be encouraged to join the management committee or become part of a pool of expertise which the project and partnerships might draw upon when needed.

Individual and collective support

Citizen advocacy projects may support advocates individually or collectively.

Providing support on an individual basis between advocate and project worker reflects the principle of the one-to-one relationship between advocate and partner to good effect. It focuses attention on that partnership alone, and allows sensitive issues to be addressed more readily.

Collective support involves meeting advocates together as a group to share problems and solutions and matters of general interest on a more or less regular basis. Some groups produce newsletters which cover issues affecting the partnerships and project. Training may also be offered to groups of advocates with shared learning needs.

In providing collective support to advocates confidentiality must be maintained. There is also a need to beware of inequality or over-professionalisation being introduced into individual partnerships through 'advocates only' meetings.

Further, there is a need to ensure that groups of advocates do not become engaged in campaigning or public advocacy under the auspices of the project. However, they may well contact particular pressure groups, such as pensioners' forums, to take up wider issues if needed.

Expenses

In supporting partnerships you should adhere to the principle of citizen advocacy being an unpaid activity. Advocates should be there because they want to be, not because they are paid to be. However, there are differing views as to whether advocacy projects should pay advocates expenses or not.

Those who oppose paying under any circumstances argue that it undermines the equality and 'ordinariness' of the partnership. On the other hand, there is a strong view within the voluntary movement as a whole that advocates should not be out of pocket as a result of their activities. There is also a risk that some people who would make good advocates might be excluded if they had to meet expenses.

On balance it is recommended that projects should offer expenses to advocates. Such expenses should be properly controlled, limited to modest or essential costs and agreed with the advocate in advance.

Partnerships in conflict

Project workers should try to identify any conflicts between advocates and partners as early as possible through follow-up or support sessions. It might be appropriate to offer direct support to the advocate, partner or both to try to resolve the situation.

Conflict should not necessarily be viewed as being a bad thing within a partnership. It can herald growth in the relationship. It may also be a sign of the tension which is part of being alongside another person without imposing one's own views.

If a conflict is causing particular unhappiness and distress for the advocate or partner and cannot be reconciled, the partnership should be ended. The partnership has been entered into voluntarily, and the advocate or the partner may choose to end their involvement at any time. You should ensure that support is available following the break-up of a partnership if needed.

Endings

Advocacy workers should ensure that the endings of partnerships are given the same broad measure of consideration as their beginnings. Endings might come about for several different reasons, each requiring its own response and support from the project:

- irreconcilable conflict between advocate and partner;
- the advocate or partner feeling unable to deal with issues arising within the partnership;
- advocate or partner moving out of the local area;
- advocate or partner wishing to leave the partnership for non-related reasons;
- the death of an advocate or partner;
- the partner deciding that they no longer require an advocate;
- the partnership deciding that they wish to continue their relationship in terms of a friendship free of the project. In this circumstance projects need to formally ensure that the advocate and partner are both aware that at their request they will no longer receive support from the project.

'Some partnerships need a lot more support than others. Some I might not see or hear from one week or month to the next. Others I see very regularly. I've also had to put in a range of intensive support for several days for just a couple of partnerships before now. I see my role as support when needed rather than strictly supervision.'

CARLEEN, ADVOCACY WORKER

3.6 Partnerships in Action

As well as setting up frameworks for support, you will also need an awareness of the kinds of issues facing partnerships if you are to help advocates to advocate in the best interests of partners. The following scenarios give examples of such issues and explore relationships between the project and partnerships, the involvement of other agencies and key concepts including legal capacity and confidentiality in practice.

Gaining access

Amy is in hospital after a fall. Carol, her advocate, has attempted to see her but access has been blocked by the ward manager who says that Amy is'resting' and that they don't want 'busybodies interfering around here'.

Considerations:

a You should make arrangements between your project and local service agencies, including hospital trusts, regarding access to users of their services.

b Generally, people may have a right to visitors but visitors do not have a right to visit. Thus it is even more important to ensure that access for advocates is negotiated with the service agency at management level.

c Carol should be encouraged to see the hospital manager to discuss the refusal of access by the ward manager.

d Carol may make a complaint through the hospital trust complaints procedures.

e Carol may inform the local community health council (or health and social services council for Northern Ireland) about the situation.

f In Scotland, NHS patients also have access to the patient supporter system.

Finding information

Flo is physically frail and is supported at home by a lot of community care services. She has told Sam her advocate that she has been uncertain about decisions made by the Department of Social Security (DSS) about her entitlements following the death of her husband several months ago. She feels that there might have been a mistake, but doesn't know what to do about it, if anything.

Considerations:

a A number of older people are 'reluctant claimants' regarding welfare benefits. Take-up is relatively low and mistakes may go undetected.

b You should ensure that advocates are aware they can refer back to the project for useful contacts and information. Sam should ensure that Flo is willing for him to do so or they may do it together.

c You will need to have developed links with people with specialist knowledge, such as welfare rights officers, and those with other useful expertise.

d You may suggest that Sam and Flo may approach the 'expert' directly. This makes it more likely that Flo will be introduced to contacts in the wider community and less likely that the partnership will become overly dependent upon the project.

e You should ensure that advocates have been informed of the need for confidentiality. Thus Sam should only disclose to a DSS officer what Flo has previously agreed.

Being there

Tina is an advocate for Joan who has severe dementia and is living in a nursing home. Joan can be very withdrawn or preoccupied. She rarely gets into a conversation and what she does say tends to be rooted in the past. She does not seem to know where she is or who is around her. She does not appear to have any visitors apart from Tina.

Considerations:

a Joan could be in a very vulnerable position as she appears to have lost any clear expression of identity or views. Those around her may stop treating her as a 'whole' and valued person.

b Tina may need support to realise that just 'being there' with Joan, observing what is 'normal' for her, listening to what she says, spending time together, providing emotional support is worthwhile and can inform practical help when needed.

c Tina may wish to find out more about Joan in order to get a better understanding of where she is now, to try to find the best ways of communicating and to be better able to represent her interests.

d You will need to have made arrangements with service agencies regarding access to records. These will need to be compatible with the Access to Personal Files Act 1987, the Access to Health Records Act 1990 and regulations and guidance under these Acts. There are codes of practice on this issue published by the Department of Health, NHS Management Executive, Scottish Social Work Services Group and Social Services Inspectorate.

e Some workers within service agencies may try to deny access to records altogether, others might disclose much personal information all too readily. As Joan may not be able to give informed consent for this to happen, it is essential to consider the ethical aspects of such situations and determine whether there is a 'need to know' by the advocate.

f Project workers might have prepared the ground for advocates by making presentations or providing training about advocacy to the management and staff of local nursing homes.

Representing interests

Harjit is an advocate for Bill who is living at home with a lot of support from the community care services. Bill has a form of dementia which has led to a speedy 'step'-like deterioration in his mental state. Nevertheless, he has retained a strong concept of home and has suggested this is where he wants to stay. Harjit has been invited to a case conference which will review Bill's situation. A member of the social services department has suggested that Bill might require an assessment for residential care or a nursing home placement, and would like the 'consent' of the advocate.

Considerations:

a Projects should ensure that advocates are aware that being an advocate does not itself confer any new legal status. Being an advocate does not mean that an individual can give consent, sign forms or carry out legally effective acts on behalf of a partner whether that partner has the capacity to take decisions or not.

b Citizen advocacy is not about substitute decision-making but putting a partner's case and ensuring that they receive their full rights and entitlements. In doing so it is entirely appropriate that advocates should attend meetings with service providers including case conferences and reviews on behalf of or alongside their partner to ensure that the interests of their partner are heard.

c Harjit should be supported by a project worker in putting forward her knowledge of Bill's wish to remain in his own home.

d It might be appropriate for the project worker to attend the case conference alongside Harjit and Bill to provide additional support.

e You may provide training to advocates in negotiating skills and the conduct of case conferences to help in this situation.

Protecting from abuse

As suggested in Part 1 (see page 18), abuse is about mistreatment of the person. Individuals, groups or organisations may misuse their power over the life of an older person. There are several forms of abuse – physical, psychological, sexual, financial, professional and institutional.

It is very important for your project to be aware of the procedures of service agencies for dealing with abuse. You might even ensure that the role of advocacy projects is included in such procedures with your agreement. You might get help and information on issues of abuse from national bodies such as Action on Elder Abuse and the Social Services Inspectorate as well as solicitors and local service agencies themselves.

The following three scenarios illustrate responses to financial abuse, physical abuse and racism.

Financial abuse

Steven is an advocate for Dot who is physically very frail. Dot lives at home alone but receives weekly visits from her son. Steven notices that Dot has very little food in the house and seems to have problems paying bills. It becomes apparent that Dot's son collects her pension, leaves her with £5 and takes the rest for himself. Dot says that her son feels she owes it to him for the 'worry she causes' and the 'hassle of having to visit'. Dot misses the money but would rather let him have it than for him not to visit at all.

Considerations:

a You will need to be aware of the various forms of abuse, including financial abuse. You will also need to know about your local health and social services agency procedures for dealing with the abuse of older people or vulnerable adults which will control what they do if suspected abuse is reported. The Department of Social Security (Department of Health and Social Security in Northern Ireland) also has guidelines for investigating abuse by people acting as agents or appointees (see pages 111–112).

b You might judge that Steven should not confront Dot's son or inform the relevant authorities. Instead, he should develop sufficient trust and confidence within the partnership to suggest that Dot stops her son from taking the money or informs the relevant authorities herself, or that she agrees for Steven to do this for her. You should advise Steven accordingly.

c Your project might have developed an arrangement with service agencies such that it is decided to inform all potential partners that suspicion of abuse might be reported directly to the appropriate authority. Of course, as Dot does not wish to take things any further, there may be major problems which rule out doing so in this case, as Steven would have to breach his legal duty of confidentiality as well as risk destroying the trust on which the partnership is based. If, however, Dot is considered to be legally unable to make her own decisions (see pages 27–28), Steven might feel a clear duty to report her circumstances.

PHYSICAL ABUSE

Helen is an advocate for Ruby who has had a major stroke and lives with her husband who is her main carer. Helen has noticed that Ruby is often bruised around her face, neck and arms. Ruby's husband usually leaves the house as soon as Helen arrives. Helen has heard him shouting at Ruby several times as she arrives at their home. Ruby discloses to Helen that her husband has been beating her but that they 'can't live with each other or without each other'.

Considerations:

a As suggested in the previous example, you will need an awareness of abuse and the procedures of service agencies and other authorities regarding potential abuse.

b Again, there is a dilemma about whether to disclose the suspected abuse to the relevant authorities without the consent of the partner. Here the issue arises that what Helen has *seen* is not 'confidential', though statements Ruby makes to her in confidence may remain so. The suspected abuse may be disclosed, particularly where the advocate considers the partner to be unable to give or withhold her consent. As what Helen sees cannot be 'confidential', her duties may be viewed as moral or ethical rather than legal.

c Your project might judge that in situations where there is concern for 'life and limb', advocates should inform the necessary authorities despite being unable to obtain the clear agreement of their partner. If this is the case, you should have ensured that the partner was made aware that this could happen before becoming part of the partnership.

Racism

Ashok is an Asian man who has mental health problems. He lives in a local authority group home in which the other residents and staff are white. Usha is Ashok's advocate. In conversation with Usha, Ashok mentioned that staff had been saying 'silly things' about him being Asian. However, he seemed reluctant to take things further.

Considerations:

a Racism may be manifest in different ways but can be seen in terms of abuse. You will need to explore whether the social services department has suitable means of dealing with this situation within their adult protection procedures or other policies on anti-discrimination.

b People from black and minority ethnic groups may be particularly discriminated against within the mental health system. Ashok may play down racist comments as 'silly things' for fear of being labelled a troublemaker, victimised or being told that it is part of his mental health problem.

c Once more there is a need to consider requirements of maintaining trust and confidentiality against the reaction to confront the alleged abuse. This does not appear to be a 'life and limb' situation. If Ashok lacks the legal capacity to make his own decisions then the advocate may decide to report the circumstances. If Usha hears the staff abusing Ashok, or indeed other residents, she may report the abuse. Otherwise, rather than going against Ashok's wishes, Usha should continue to develop their relationship and find ways of supporting Ashok if he ever feels that he does want to take the matter further.

Self-harm

Milly has been Lynda's advocate for several months. Lynda lives at home alone. She has often seemed quite low. One day Lynda told Milly that she had been stockpiling tablets prescribed by the GP for some time and was intending to commit suicide.

Considerations:

a You will need to be able to offer a good deal of support from the project directly or indirectly through professional allies in the community. Milly might be encouraged to ask 'Why has Lynda told me this?' and 'What am I expected to do with the information?'.

b It would be illegal for Milly to assist Lynda with any attempt she might make upon her own life.

c Milly might suggest to Lynda where she could get help. She might also try to establish whether Lynda is so unwell as to be unable to make a real choice.

d There is no legal obligation to report the situation. However, the project may need to be aware of when mental health legislation can be employed to assess or treat a person with mental health problems, and the very limited circumstances in which such legislation can be enforced. Where they are clearly applicable it may be considered necessary and right for the circumstances to be reported to Lynda's doctor.

3.7 Legal Roles

Advocates may acquire specific legal status, rights and responsibilities in terms of the roles outlined in this section. All these roles can be performed by someone other than an advocate, but in many cases an advocate will be a very suitable person to take on formal responsibility. You should have access to legal expertise and be able to support advocates who acquire such status.

Advocates may also work alongside another person who holds specific legal status, such as a solicitor or member of the social services department, in the interests of their partner. Again, you should be able to support the advocate in this task.

Agency

A partner who is in receipt of a state retirement pension or other state benefits may nominate their advocate to collect the benefit for them and sign their order book accordingly. This allows the advocate to collect their partner's state benefits from the local post office. The advocate cannot spend this money or keep it without specific instruction or authority. The duty of the advocate as agent is simply to give the money to their partner once collected on their behalf. Control of the money remains with the partner. There are special social security arrangements where the advocate may become an agent on a long-term basis. Agency cannot be used where the partner lacks the legal capacity to give authorisations or instructions.

Appointee

An advocate may become an appointee, able to make claims for, receive and deal with state benefits on behalf of their partner. In order to do so, the advocate needs to apply to the local Department of Social Security (DSS) office (Department of Health and Social Services in Northern Ireland). Social security regulations state that the claimant must be 'unable for the time being to act'. This usually means that the partner does not have the mental capacity to look after his or her financial affairs, because of dementia, disease, or learning disability. Occasionally, the problem might be temporary, for example because of a serious accident.

The advocate must demonstrate to the DSS that they would make the most suitable appointee and show an active interest in the welfare of their partner. If accepted, the advocate will have a duty to ensure that the partner will get the full benefit of the payment made and that any changes in the circumstances of the partner which may affect their benefits are promptly reported.

Appointment under the Social Security Regulations comes to an end if it is revoked by the DSS; if the appointee resigns after giving one month's notice; or if the DSS is told that a receiver has been appointed by the Court of Protection for England and Wales, or in Scotland a curator bonis (or other judicial factor) has been appointed by the Sheriff Court or Court of Session, or in Northern Ireland the High Court appoints a controller of the person. The DSS must also be notified if either the claimant or the appointee dies.

'Appointeeship can be beneficial to the development of partnerships in requiring there to be a regular contact. It can be of real benefit to partners living in institutional settings as the money remains with and is put to best use for the individual instead of being pooled with others or held by proprietors.' VIC, ADVOCACY WORKER

POWER OF ATTORNEY

A power of attorney is an arrangement by which one individual (the donor) gives authority to another or others (the attorney/s or donee/s) to act on his or her behalf. The attorney is required to act as if she or he were the donor. Appointing an attorney might be a good idea if the partner has difficulty getting out to the bank or building society, or has difficulty signing cheques or documents. However, power of attorney (like agency) cannot be used where the partner does not have the mental capacity to give authorisation to the attorney.

The power can be used in specific or general areas of managing income and capital. Copies can be shown to banks, building societies, pension funds or insurance and pensions companies when required. At any time the donor can cancel the power of attorney. The attorney must demonstrate that they are taking proper care of the donor's affairs and may be sued for any loss due to insufficient care.

It is very important to realise that in England, Wales and Northern Ireland a power of attorney is automatically cancelled by operation of law when the partner loses mental capacity to manage his or her own affairs. An attorney who then continues to act is doing so without authority and is liable to be sued. Instead, the attorney should stop acting. The partner's affairs may then have to be handled by the Court of Protection in England and Wales or the High Court and the Office of Care and Protection in Northern Ireland.

In Scotland it is possible to have a continuing power of attorney which is still valid even if the person loses capacity. The original document should state whether or not it continues after capacity, but there does not have to be a special form like the enduring power of attorney (see below), and the deed does not have to be specially registered.

'Power of attorney depends upon ongoing consent and trust. It reflects the basis of a citizen advocacy partnership where the partner is capable of giving consent and understanding the nature of the relationship. It requires regular contact between partner and advocate if the advocate is to be seen to be adequately undertaking their role as an attorney. In the absence of others, power of attorney may seem better held by the advocate than anyone connected, say, with management of residential care homes and nursing homes.'

SHEILA, PROJECT WORKER.

ENDURING POWER OF ATTORNEY

Unlike an ordinary power of attorney, in England, Wales and Northern Ireland an enduring power of attorney (EPA) can continue in force even if the individual loses mental capacity. EPAs are often made by older people who are aware of failing mental faculties, but still have capacity to understand what is involved in creating an EPA. The EPA can give the attorney general power to act in relation to the donor's property and affairs, or can relate to specific items. An EPA must be made in a prescribed form laid down by law, and the partner will probably have to consult a solicitor or legal adviser. Whilst it is more usual for a solicitor or social services department to act as an attorney under an EPA, it could be appropriate for an advocate to do so at the request of their partner.

An attorney under an EPA must take proper care of the donor's affairs and also takes on certain special duties. As soon as the attorney believes that the donor is or is becoming mentally incapable then the attorney must stop acting until the EPA has been registered by the Court of Protection in England and Wales or by the High Court in Northern Ireland. Again, this must be done in the correct prescribed form, with certain relatives of the donor (laid down by law) being informed. Once the EPA is registered, the attorney can safely start acting again.

'Although EPAs seem useful in that they continue to be in force even where the person loses mental capacity, in practice there are difficulties for partnerships where the advocate is a potential attorney. There is a time-lag in getting an EPA and circumstances can change in the meantime. In the early days of a partnership it might not be certain how things will work out, so it needs careful thought before being pursued.'

WENDY, MANAGEMENT COMMITTEE MEMBER

Court of Protection

In England and Wales the Court of Protection (address on page 134) exists to protect the interests of people who are unable to manage their own financial affairs because of mental disorder. The term 'mental disorder' is a legal label which includes dementia, learning disabilities and mental health problems.

The Court usually delegates power over the income of the patient to a 'receiver' who can handle day-to-day matters. Capital is usually retained on deposit by the Court. Anyone can apply to be a receiver, giving full details of the patient's finances and family situation (and paying the Court fee). Often a relative or solicitor applies, but it would be appropriate for an advocate to do so.

The responsibilities of the receiver are detailed in a handbook issued by the Court. The receiver is required to handle all financial transactions for the benefit of the person. Their dealings are monitored by the Court which requires the submission of annual accounts. An annual fee is usually payable to the Court of Protection.

In Northern Ireland, the interests of people who are unable to manage their own financial affairs because of mental disorder are looked after by the High Court and the Office of Care and Protection. The High Court may delegate power over the income of the patient to a 'controller' whose powers are the same as those of a receiver.

As a receiver, an advocate could be well placed to meet the partner's needs and interests. Advocates are independent so do not have the same vested interests as others may hold. They are only concerned with their partner as an individual and can concentrate on ensuring that their partner's affairs are handled in the best interests of their partner alone. However, as there are costs involved, the project will need to consider carefully how it might support partnerships in such arrangements and advocates need to consider the degree of responsibility it entails.

'I looked into becoming a receiver for Les, my partner. It is a highly responsible role, with costs involved. I felt that it would be better for me to work alongside a solicitor who is now the receiver. I feel that I can help to inform how the money is spent as I have a closer relationship with Les than the solicitor does. The solicitor usually agrees with me anyway – we both want the best for Les.' George, Advocate.

Curator bonis (Scotland only)

If a person is unable to manage their financial affairs due to mental disorder, a curator bonis can be appointed. The appointment is made by the Sheriff Court on the basis of two medical reports. The curator takes over full responsibility for handling the person's finances and is required to follow detailed rules and act under the supervision of the Accountant of Court.

Because the procedure is fairly complex, the curator is usually a professional such as a solicitor. An advocate could conceivably become a curator, but it is more likely that they would play a role in ensuring that the curator was taking proper account of the person's needs and wishes. Since a curatory is often expensive and cumbersome, another role might be to ensure that alternatives such as trusts are explored.

'I'm finding my way around the system to ensure that Muriel is getting the best deal possible. I don't have a list of clients, I'm just here for her. I make sure that the curator, who is a solicitor, is fully in the picture before I leave.'

TRISHA, ADVOCATE

TUTOR DATIVE (SCOTLAND ONLY)

A tutor dative is a kind of personal guardian. There is no English equivalent. The tutor can exercise a range of powers on behalf of a person who is unable to act because of mental disorder. The powers can include deciding where a person should live, consenting on their behalf to medical treatment, deciding who should have access to a person, and initiating medical treatment. The Court will decide, based on the person's degree of disability and circumstances.

Tutors are usually relatives, but others can be appointed. Strictly, they are decision-makers, not advocates. However, many tutors see the value of the appointment as giving them a 'voice' and status with service providers.

'It is possible that the tutor dative procedure could be developed to allow people to be granted specific advocacy powers, for example to speak for, advise and represent the person with a mental disorder.' BEN, LEGAL ADVOCATE

Guardianship

Under the Mental Health Act 1983 in England and Wales and the Mental Health (Scotland) Act 1984, a person who has one of four specified forms of 'mental disorder' may be received into guardianship if it is necessary for their own welfare or the protection of others. The guardian will almost always be the local social services authority as this form of 'guardianship' is a way of seeking compulsory control over a person who needs help. The guardian has the power to require the individual to live at a particular place, to attend particular places for medical treatment, occupation or training, and to require access to be given to doctors, social workers and others at any place where she or he resides. Application for guardianship is made to the local authority and must be supported by two doctors and an approved social worker or in Scotland a mental health officer.

Under the Mental Health (Northern Ireland) Order 1987, a person who has one of two specified forms of mental disorder may be received into guardianship if it is necessary for his own welfare. The guardian is generally the local health and social services board. The guardian has the same powers as in England and Wales. Application for guardianship is made to the local health and social services board, usually by an approved social worker, and must be accompanied by two medical recommendations and a recommendation by an approved social worker who is not the person making the application.

'It is hard to imagine circumstances in which it would be appropriate for an advocate to act as a Mental Health Act guardian to their partner. It is more likely that the advocate would become involved alongside a social worker or other person acting as guardian. They would, for instance, monitor how their partner was being treated, provide useful information, and support their partner in making realistic choices.'

Peter, Advocacy Worker

Advance statements about health care ('living wills')

A partner with a progressive illness which could lead to loss of decision-making capacity in the future may wish to record his or her views about health care options. This might cover issues concerning refusal of treatment, requests for treatment and purposes of treatment. If the partner then loses capacity and cannot participate in health care decisions, those involved in treatment and care would be able to take the previously-expressed views into account. If the views are written down then the document is often called an 'advance directive' or 'living will'.

There is no reason why partners should not also record wishes and feelings about other aspects of life, such as whether to go into residential care. Although it is not clear what the legal status of such a document would be, it would present a good opportunity for partner and advocate to discuss matters and the advocate might later find it very useful.

There is no legislation about living wills in the United Kingdom. There is some relevant English case law regarding advance decisions to refuse particular treatment. However, there are many complex considerations and interests involved and the position is not clear in every possible situation.

Rather than making any formal arrangements through a solicitor, a partner may simply want to have a proper discussion with the health care team and to record their general wishes and feelings about future treatment. Sometimes it is difficult for a person to initiate such a dialogue and an advocate may then encourage and support them in their discussions.

If a partner wishes to make a formal living will or advance directive, then the advocate and your project should be able to support them in doing so. The partner should neither feel pressurised into nor put off from going through with the exercise.

There are several possible sources of help. A variety of organisations publish blank forms – one of the simplest and most successful is produced by the Terrence Higgins Trust. The Exchange on Ageing, Law and Ethics (EAGLE) is a useful network of interested professionals and organisations which publishes a bimonthly journal. The British Medical Association is expected to publish a code of practice on advance directives during 1995.

Law reform

The Law Commission for England and Wales has been examining the law relating to decision-making on behalf of mentally incapacitated adults (see Consultation Papers Nos 119, 128, 129 and 130). The Commission reported to the Lord Chancellor in March 1995, with recommendations for law reform. Their provisional proposals included the extension of enduring powers of attorney to personal and health care decisions and a new jurisdiction for the court or a court-appointed manager to take decisions on behalf of another person. They also proposed that there should be legislation to regulate advance directives for health care.

The Scottish Law Commission is undertaking its own examination of the law relating to decision-making on behalf of mentally incapacitated adults (see Discussion Papers 94 and 96). The Commission is to report to the Secretary of State for Scotland. There is no similar law reform exercise being carried out in Northern Ireland.

If legislation is enacted, this Code will be updated to include it.

3.8 Part 3 Further Reading

Butler, K *et al* (1988) *Citizen Advocacy: A powerful partnership*. National Citizen Advocacy (now Citizen Advocacy Information and Training), London.

Counsel and Care (1992) *What if they Hurt Themselves? A discussion document on the uses and abuses of restraint in residential care and nursing homes for older people*. Counsel and Care, London.

Eastman, M (ed) (1994, 2nd edition) *Old Age Abuse: A new perspective*. Chapman Hall/Age Concern England, London.

Forrest, A (1986) *Citizen Advocacy: Including the excluded*. Sheffield Citizen Advocacy, Sheffield.

Greengross, S (1986) *The Law and Vulnerable Elderly People*. Age Concern England, London.

Holly, L and Webb, B (1992) *Advocacy in Practice: (1) Co-ordinating advocacy (2) Advocates' experiences*. Evaluation, Development and Review Unit, Tavistock Centre, London.

Ivers, V (1994) *Citizen Advocacy in Action: Working with older people*. Beth Johnson Foundation, Stoke on Trent.

Marshall, M (ed) (1990) *Working with Dementia: Guidelines for professionals*. Venture Press, Birmingham.

Meredith, B (1993) *The Community Care Handbook: The new system explained*. Age Concern England, London.

Paterson, J (20th edition, 1995) *Disability Rights Handbook*. Disability Alliance ERA, London

Simons, K (1994) *Citizen Advocacy: An inside view*. Norah Fry Institute, Bristol.

PART 4

Getting Help

Although citizen advocacy is mainly concerned with local community networks, there can be great benefits in making contacts on a regional and national scale.

Part 4 lists a variety of groups and organisations that are relevant to citizen advocacy projects with older people in the UK.

4.1 Citizen Advocacy and Related Advocacy Projects with Older People

You may seek to build networks with other citizen advocacy and related advocacy projects involved with older people to share information and support. These include:

Age Concern Carlisle Advocacy Project
3 Chatsworth Square
Carlisle
Cumbria CA1 1HB
Tel: 01228 36673

Bath Age Concern Citizen Advocacy
c/o St Martins Hospital
Bath BA2 5RP

Bedfordshire Advocacy Alliance
41 Mill Street
Bedford
Bedfordshire MK40 3EU
Tel: 01234 262080

Berkshire Alzheimer's Disease Society Advocacy Scheme
10 Gun Street
Reading
Berkshire RG1 2JR
Tel: 01734 580040

Beth Johnson Foundation
North Staffordshire Advocacy
and Older People Project
Parkfield House
64 Princes Road
Hartshill
Stoke on Trent ST4 7JL

Tel: 01782 44036

Bexley ACE Advocacy Project
Room 201
Erith and District Hospital
Park Crescent
Erith
Kent DA8 3EE

Tel: 01322 335670

Birmingham Citizen Advocacy
Southside
249 Ladypool Road
Sparkbrook
Birmingham B12 8LF

Tel: 0121 440 2029

Brighton and Hove MIND Advocacy Project for Mental Health Service Users Over 65
79 Buckingham Road
Brighton
East Sussex BN1 3RT

Tel: 01273 749600

Bromley Advocacy Project
St Mary's Church House
61 College Road
Bromley
Kent BR1 3QG

Tel: 0181 313 0139

Camden Age Concern Advocacy Project
Bramber Green Centre
Wakefield Road
London WC1N 1PG

Tel: 0171 837 6317

Cheshire Age Concern Advocacy Project
Trinity
Riseley Street
Macclesfield
Cheshire SK10 1BW

Tel: 01625 619131

Citizen Advocacy Alliance
6 Lind Road
Sutton
Surrey SM1 4PJ

Tel: 0181 643 7111

(Primarily learning disability)

Connect Advocacy Project
Continuing Care
Hackney Hospital
Homerton High Street
London E9 6BE

Tel: 0181 919 8176

Cumbernauld Action on Care of the Elderly
c/o Alpha Project
Muirfield Centre
Brown Road
Cumbernauld G67 1AA

Tel: 01236 451393

East Sussex Age Concern Advocacy Project
143 High Street
Lewes
East Sussex BN7 1NT

Tel: 01273 476704

Fife Advocacy Project
Office 3
Millie Street
Kirkcaldy
Fife KY1 2NL
Tel: 01592 640694

Gateshead Alzheimer's Disease Society Advocacy Scheme
John Haswell House
8–9 Gladstone Terrace
Tyne and Wear NE8 4DY
Tel: 0191 477 7490

Gloucestershire Age Concern Advocacy Project
Jubilee Suite
Grosvenor House
Station Road
Gloucester GL1 1SZ
Tel: 01452 309888

Hertfordshire Advocacy Development Project
Mentmore
Church Crescent
St Albans
Hertfordshire AL3 5JB
Tel: 01727 848529

Isle of Wight Advocacy Consortium
34 The Mall
Carisbrooke Road
Newport
Isle of Wight PO30 1BW
Tel: 01983 528827

Kent Age Concern Advocacy Project
Citizens' Rights for Older People
4 Hilary Road
Penenden Heath
Maidstone
Kent ME14 2JP
Tel: 01622 679863

Kingston Citizen Advocacy Group
Richard Mayo Hall
Eden Street
Kingston-upon-Thames
Surrey KT1 1HZ
Tel: 0181 549 1028

Leeds Age Concern Citizen Advocacy Project
188A Woodhouse Lane
Leeds LS2 9DX
Tel: 01532 458579

Lurgan Hospital Advocacy Scheme
(Age Concern Northern Ireland)
8 Sloan Street
Lurgan
County Armagh BT66 8NX
Tel: 01762 323266

Newcastle Age Concern Citizen Advocacy Project
Mea House
Ellison Place
Newcastle upon Tyne NE1 8XS
Tel: 0191 232 6488

North East Glasgow and Strathkelvin Advocacy Project
Room 3
Southbank House
Southbank Business Park
Kirkintilloch
Glasgow G66 1XQ

Tel: 0141 775 0433

Nottingham Alzheimer's Disease Society Advocacy Project
CVS
33 Mansfield Road
Nottingham NG1 3FF

Tel: 01159 859094

Nottinghamshire Age Concern Advocacy Scheme
Woodland Chambers
52A Long Row
Nottingham NG1 6JB

Tel: 01602 475892

Oxfordshire Advocacy Development Group
Wallingford Hospital
Reading Road
Wallingford
Oxfordfordshire OX10 9DU

Tel: 01491 824600

Scarborough, Whitby, Filey and Ryedale Advocacy Alliance
Allatt House
5 West Parade Road
Scarborough
North Yorkshire YO12 5ED

Tel: 01723 363910

Somali Elders Befriending Project
c/o Liverpool Personal Service Society
18 Seel Street
Liverpool L1 4BE

Tel: 0151 707 0131

South Glamorgan Age Concern Advocacy Project
91–93 Caerphilly Road
Birchgrove
Cardiff CF4 4AE

Tel: 01222 521052

South Warwickshire Independent Advocacy Alliance
The Advocacy Office
19 Waterloo Place
Leamington Spa CV32 5LA

Tel: 01926 887990

SPEAK
c/o Age Concern Kingstanding
Seymour Day Centre
Princess Alice Drive
Chester Road North
Birmingham B73 6RD

Tel: 0121 354 4301

Tendring Advocacy Scheme for Elderly People
Hurlingham Chambers
61–65 Station Road
Clacton on Sea
Essex CO15 1AS

Tel: 0255 435095

Wakefield Age Concern Independent Support Project
29 Cornmarket
Pontefract
West Yorkshire WF8 1BJ

Tel: 01977 706751

Wessex Advocacy Consortium (CHOICES)
18 Oxford Street
Southampton SO14 3DJ
Tel: 01703 228291

Westminster Advocacy for Older People
284 Harrow Road
London W2 5ES
Tel: 0171 266 4207

Wolverhampton Age Concern Advocacy Project
Blossoms Fold
93–94 Darlington Street
Wolverhampton WV1 4EX
Tel: 01902 711232

4.2 Pensioners' Forums and Related Organisations

You may develop alliances with pensioners' forums and related organisations. These are groups of older people for older people. They aim to provide a voice for older people and raise awareness about relevant issues. They include:

England

Age Concern Liverpool Consumer Council
Sir Thomas House
5 Sir Thomas Street
Liverpool L1 6BW
Tel: 0151 236 4440

Association of Greater London Older Women
Manor Garden Centre
6–9 Manor Gardens
London N7 6LA

Elderly Voices, Nottingham
c/o The Council House
Nottingham NG1 2DT

Greater London Forum for the Elderly
54 Chalton Street
London NW1 1JR
Tel: 0171 383 4008

Greater London Pensioners' Association
28a Highgate Road
London NW5 1NS

Leicester Senior Citizens' Sub-Committee
c/o Leicester City Council
New Walk Centre
Welford Place
Leicester LE1 6ZG
Tel: 01533 545531

Mansfield Pensioners' Action Association
c/o 25 Bakewell Walk
Mansfield
Nottinghamshire NG18 3PY

Merseyside Pensioners' Association
5 Alder Crescent
Kirkby
Merseyside L32 0SB
Tel: 0151 546 6743

Norfolk and Norwich Pensioners' Association
c/o 2 Williams Close
Wymondham
Norfolk NR18 0DT

North East Pensioners' Association
c/o SEARCH
74 Adelaide Terrace
Benwell
Newcastle upon Tyne NE4 9JN

North Staffordshire Pensioners' Convention
c/o 4 Broad Street
Hanley
Stoke on Trent
Staffordshire ST1 4HL
Tel: 01782 201724

North West Pensioners' Association
c/o 34 Langworthy Road
Salford
Manchester M6 5SH
Tel: 0161 736 5485

Older Feminists' Network
54 Gordon Road
London N3 1EP

Oxfordshire Pensioners' Action Group
c/o 94 Ridgefield Road
Oxford OX4 3DA

Sheffield Pensioners' Action Group
c/o 11–12 North Gallery
Castle Market Building
Exchange Street
Sheffield S2 5TS

Suffolk Pensioners' Association
c/o 32 High Street
Ipswich IP1 3QJ

Standing Conference of Ethnic Minority Senior Citizens (London)
5 Westminster Bridge Road
London SE1 7XW
Tel: 0171 928 0095

West Midlands Pensioners' Convention
c/o 37 Woodfield Road
Moseley
Birmingham B13 9UL

Northern Ireland

Action Age
c/o Age Concern Northern Ireland
3 Lower Crescent
Belfast BT7 1NR
Tel: 01232 245729

Scotland

Dumfries and Galloway Elderly Forum
c/o Dialknowe
Wanlockhead
Biggar ML12 6UY

Fife Elderly Forum
Office 2
Fraser Buildings
Millie Street
Kirkcaldy
Fife KY1 2NL
Tel: 01592 643743

Scottish Old Age Pensions Association
c/o 34 Queensway
Penicuik
Midlothian EH26 0JE

The Scottish Pensioners' Forum
Middleton House
Woodlands Terrace
Glasgow G3 6DF
Tel: 0141 332 4946

Strathclyde Elderly Forum
Block 6, Unit E2
Templeton Business Centre
Glasgow G40 1DA
Tel: 0141 551 0595

Wales

Eastern Senior Citizens' Association
Woodcroft Resource Centre
for the Elderly
Glan-Y-Mor Road
Trowbridge
Cardiff CF3 8RP

East Vale Pensioners' Forum
c/o 28 Caerleon Road
Dinas Powys
South Glamorgan CF4 4AE

South Glamorgan County Pensioners' Action Forum
c/o 91–93 Caerphilly Road
Birchgrove
Cardiff CF4 4AE

Nationwide Organisations

British Pensioners and Trade Union Action Association
315 Bexley Road
Erith
Kent DA8 3EZ
Tel: 01322 335464

National Federation of Retirement Pensioners' Associations (Pensioners' Voice)
14 St Peter Street
Blackburn
Lancashire BB2 2HD
Tel: 01254 52606

National Pensioners' Convention
c/o 4 Stevens Street
Lowestoft
Suffolk NR32 2JE

Pensioners' Rights Campaign
Hartington Place
Carlisle
Cumbria CA1 1HL

4.3 Other Advocacy and Advocacy-related Organisations

You may seek to make links with other advocacy and advocacy-related organisations which promote and provide advice, information, support and training on advocacy issues.

Association of Community Health Councils for England and Wales
30 Drayton Park
London N5 1PB
Tel: 0171 609 8405

British Council of Organisations of Disabled People
Litchurch Plaza
Litchurch Lane
Derby DE24 8AA
Tel: 01332 295551

British Deaf Association
38 Victoria Place
Carlisle CA1 1HU
Tel: 01228 48844

Citizen Advocacy Information and Training
(formerly NCA)
Unit 2K
Leroy House
436 Essex Road
London N1 3QP
Tel: 0171 359 8289

Disability Action (Northern Ireland)
2 Annadale Avenue
Belfast BT7 3JR
Tel: 01232 491011
(Forum, support, information)

Disability Alliance
Universal House
88 Wentworth Street
London E1 7SA
Tel: 0171 247 8776
Rights Line: 0171 247 8763
(Information, research, campaigns)

Exchange on Ageing, Law and Ethics (EAGLE)
c/o Age Concern England
1268 London Road
London SW16 4ER
Tel: 0181 679 8000
(Network and journal on legal rights and issues)

GLAD (Greater London Association of Disabled People)
336 Brixton Road
London SW9 7AA
Tel: 0171 274 0107
(Information, publications, campaigns. Self advocacy)

Law Centres Federation
Duchess House
18–19 Warren Street
London W1P 5DB
Tel: 0171 387 8570
(Forum, information, representation)

National Advocacy Working Party
c/o Sheffield Citizen Advocacy Project
Unit 39, Aizlewoods Mill
Nursery Street
Sheffield S3 8GG

(Forum, network)

National Association of Citizens Advice Bureaux
Myddleton House
115–123 Pentonville Road
London N1 9LZ

Tel: 0171 833 2181

National Consumer Council
20 Grosvenor Gardens
London SW1W 0DH

Tel: 0171 730 3469

(Forum, information, publications)

National Federation of the Blind
Unity House
Smyth Street
Wakefield
West Yorkshire WF1 1ER

Tel: 01924 291313

(Representation, campaigns)

National Tenants' Organisation
The Voluntary Action Centre
18 School Road
Hounslow
Middlesex TW3 1QN

Tel: 0181 569 5823

(Representation, information, training, lobbying, publications)

One-to-One
404 Camden Road
London N7 0SJ

Tel: 0171 700 5574

(Advocacy rooted in friendship. Learning disabilities)

Open Services Project
Tempo House
15 Falcon Road
London SW11 2PJ

Tel: 0171 228 0085

(Citizen involvement, user participation)

Patients' Association
8 Guildford Street
London WC1N 1DT

Tel: 0171 242 3460

(Representation, information, patients' forum)

People First
Instrument House
207–215 Kings Cross Road
London WC1X 9DB

Tel: 0171 713 6400

(Self advocacy. Learning disabilities)

Royal Association for Disability and Rehabilitation (RADAR)
12 City Forum
250 City Road
London EC1V 8AF

Tel: 0171 250 3222

(Campaigns, information)

Scotland Patients' Association
Gartincaber Farm
West Plean
Stirling FK7 8BA

Tel: 01786 818008

Scottish Association of Health Councils
5 Leamington Terrace
Edinburgh EH10 4JW

Tel: 0131 229 2344

Scottish Consumer Council
Royal Exchange House
100 Queen Street
Glasgow G1 3DN

Tel: 0141 226 5261

South Wales Advocacy Network
c/o Citizen Advocacy in South Glamorgan
43 Charles Street
Cardiff CF1 4EB

(Forum, generic)

Standing Conference on Citizen Advocacy for Wales
c/o Mongomeryshire Citizen Advocacy Project
Office 1, The Courtyard
Severn Street
Newtown
Powys SY16 2AQ

Tel: 01686 629951

(Forum, generic)

Survivors Speak Out
34 Osnaburgh Street
London NW1 3ND

Tel: 0171 916 5472

(Self advocacy. Mental health)

UK Advocacy Network (UKAN)
Premier House
14 Burgess Street
Sheffield S1 2HG

Tel: 01742 753131

(Mental health. Self advocacy)

Values into Action
Oxford House
Derbyshire Street
London E2 6HG

Tel: 0171 729 5436

(Promotion of good practice. Learning disabilities)

Welsh Consumer Council
Castle Buildings
Womanby Street
Cardiff CF1 2BW

Tel: 01222 396056

4.4 Service Agencies and Professional Associations

Whilst adhering to the principle of independence, you may choose to develop contacts with service agencies and professional organisations in order to raise awareness of advocacy issues and make useful allies.

Some of the organisations who have supported the development of advocacy projects include:

Age Concern Cymru
4th Floor
1 Cathedral Road
Cardiff CF1 9SD

Tel: 01222 371566

Age Concern England
1268 London Road
London SW16 4ER

Tel: 0181 679 8000

Age Concern Northern Ireland
3 Lower Crescent
Belfast BT7 1NR

Tel: 01232 245729

Age Concern Scotland
113 Rose Street
Edinburgh EH2 3DT

Tel: 0131 220 3345

Alzheimer's Disease Society
Gordon House
10 Greencoat Place
London SW1P 1PH

Tel: 0171 306 0606

Alzheimer Scotland – Action on Dementia
8 Hill Street
Edinburgh EH2 3JZ

Tel: 0131 220 6155

Advice: 0131 220 6155

British Association of Social Workers
16 Kent Street
Birmingham B5 6RD

Tel: 0121 622 3911

British Medical Association
BMA House
Tavistock Square
London WC1H 9JP

Tel: 0171 387 4499

Enable
6th Floor
7 Buchanan Street
Glasgow G1 3HL

Tel: 0141 226 4541

(Learning disabilities)

Help the Aged
St James Walk
London EC1R 0BE

Tel: 0171 253 0253
Freephone advice line
Seniorline: 0800 289404

Leonard Cheshire Foundation
26–29 Maunsel Street
London SW1P 2QN

Tel: 0171 828 1822

(Mental health. Disability. Learning disabilities)

Mencap
123 Golden Lane
London EC1Y 0RT
Tel: 0171 454 0454
(Learning disabilities)

Methodist Homes for the Aged
Epworth House
Stuart Street
Derby DE1 2EQ
Tel: 01332 296200

MIND
Granta House
15–19 Broadway
Stratford
London E15 4BQ
Tel: 0181 519 2122
(Mental health)

National Institute for Social Work
5–7 Tavistock Place
London WC1H 9SN
Tel: 0171 387 9681

National Schizophrenia Fellowship
28 Castle Street
Kingston upon Thames
Surrey KT1 1SS
Tel: 0181 547 3937

Northern Ireland Association for Mental Health (MIND)
80 University Street
Belfast BT7 1HE
Tel: 01232 328474

Royal College of Nursing
20 Cavendish Square
London W1M 0AB
Tel: 0171 409 3333

Royal National Institute for Deaf People
105 Gower Street
London WC1E 6AH
Tel: 0171 387 8033

SENSE (National Deaf Blind and Rubella Association)
11–13 Clifton Terrace
London N4 3SR
Tel: 0171 272 7774

SCOPE
12 Park Crescent
London W1N 4EQ
Tel: 0171 636 5020
(Cerebral palsy)

Scottish Association for Mental Health
Atlantic House
38 Garner's Crescent
Edinburgh EH3 8DQ
Tel: 0131 229 9687

Social Care Association
23A Victoria Road
Surbiton
Surrey KT6 4JZ
Tel: 0181 390 6831

Stroke Association
CHSA House
123–127 Whitecross Street
London EC1Y 8JJ
Tel: 0171 490 7999

4.5 Other Useful Addresses

You may try to build links with a variety of organisations which provide information and other resources which could be relevant to your activities, including:

ACAS (Advisory, Conciliation and Arbitration Service)
27 Wilton Street
London SW1X 7AZ

Tel: 0171 210 3000

ACRE (Action with Communities in Rural England)
Somerford Court
Somerford Road
Cirencester
Gloucestershire GL7 1TW

Tel: 01285 653477

(Forum, representation, information, publications)

Action on Elder Abuse
Astral House
1268 London Road
London SW16 4ER

Tel: 0181 679 8000

(Information, advice, promotes good practice)

Age Resource
c/o Age Concern England
1268 London Road
London SW16 4ER

Tel: 0181 679 8000

(Information, training)

British Association for Service to the Elderly (BASE)
119 Hassell Street
Newcastle under Lyme
Staffordshire

Tel: 01782 661033

(Education, training, research)

British Insurance Brokers Association
Biba House
Bevis Marks
London EC3A 7NT

Tel: 0171 623 9043

Care and Repair
Castle House
Kirtley Drive
Nottingham NG7 1LD

Tel: 01602 799091

(Information, training and support for home improvement. Disability. Older People)

Carers National Association
20–25 Glasshouse Yard
London EC1A 4JS

Tel: 0171 490 8818

(Information, support, campaigning)

Carers National Association Northern Ireland
Regional Office
113 University Street
Belfast BT7 1HP

Tel: 01232 439 843

Centre for Policy on Ageing
25–31 Ironmonger Row
London EC1V 3QP

Tel: 0171 253 1787

(Promotes good practice. Information, research, publications)

Charities Aid Foundation
48 Pembury Road
Tonbridge
Kent TN9 2JD

Tel: 01732 771333

(Information, funding, publications)

Charity Commission
St Alban's House
57 Haymarket
London SW1Y 4QX

Tel: 0171 210 3000

Commission for Racial Equality
Elliott House
10–12 Allington Street
London SW1E 5EH

Tel: 0171 828 7022

Community Matters (formerly National Federation of Community Organisations)
8–9 Upper Street
London N1 0PQ

Tel: 0171 226 0189

(Umbrella group. Information, advice)

Consortium on Opportunities for Volunteering
Carriage Row
183 Eversholt Street
London NW1 1BU

Tel: 0171 383 0441

(Funding)

Counsel and Care
Twyman House
16 Bonny Street
London NW1 9PG

Tel: 0171 485 1566

(Telephone counselling, advice, financial information, publications. Older People)

Court of Protection
Protection Division
Public Trust Office
Stewart House
24 Kingsway
London WC2B 6JX

Tel: 0171 269 7157/7358/7317

Data Protection Registrar
Wycliffe House
Water Lane
Wilmslow
Cheshire FK9 5AF

Tel: 01625 535777

DIAL UK
St Catherine's Hospital
Tickhill Road
Balby
Doncaster DN4 8QN

Tel: 01302 310123

(Helpline. Advice, information, counselling. Disability issues)

Department of Employment
Caxton House
Tothill Street
London SW1H 9NF

Tel: 0171 273 6969

Department of Finance and Personnel (Northern Ireland)
Parliament Buildings
Stormont
Belfast BT4 3SW

Tel: 01232 520000

Department of Health
Wellington House
133–155 Waterloo Road
London SE1 8UG

Tel: 0171 972 2000

Department of Health and Social Services (Northern Ireland)
Dundonald House
Upper Newtownards Road
Belfast BT4 3SF

Tel: 01232 520000

Department of Social Security
The Adelphi
1–11 John Adam Street
London WC2N 6HT

Tel: 0171 962 8000

DSS benefits advice
Seniorline: 0800 289404

Directory of Social Change
Radius Works
Back Lane
London NW3 1HL

Tel: 0171 284 4364

(Information, publications)

Disabled Living Foundation
380–384 Harrow Road
London W9 2HU

Tel: 0171 289 6111

(Information, advice, aids, equipment, publications)

Equal Opportunities Commission
Overseas House
Quay Street
Manchester M3 3HN

Tel: 0161 833 9244

Equal Opportunities Commission for Northern Ireland
Chamber of Commerce House
22 Great Victoria Street
Belfast BT2 7BA

Tel: 01232 242752

Fair Employment Commission (Northern Ireland)
Andras House
60 Great Victoria Street
Belfast BT2 7BB

Tel: 01232 240020

Federation of Independent Advice Centres (FIAC)
13 Stockwell Road
London SW9 9AU

Tel: 0171 274 1839

(Forum, information, training, support services)

Financial Intermediaries and Claims Office (Charity Division)
St John's House
Merton Road
Stanley Precinct
Bootle
Merseyside L69 4EJ

Tel: 0151 472 6038

(Inland Revenue. Tax exemptions, including Northern Ireland)

Good Practices in Mental Health
380–384 Harrow Road
London W9 2HU

Tel: 0171 289 2034/3060

(Promotes good practice. Information, publications, training)

Health and Safety Executive
The Information Centre
Broad Lane
Sheffield S3 7HQ

Tel: 01142 892345

High Court (Northern Ireland)
Royal Court of Justice
Chichester Street
Belfast BT1 3JU

Tel: 01232 235111

King's Fund
126 Albert Street
London NW1 7NF

Tel: 0171 267 6111

(Promotes good practice in health and social care. Information, research, funding)

Law Commission
Conquest House
37–38 John Street
Theobalds Road
London WC1N 2BQ

Tel: 0171 411 1220

Law Commission (Scotland)
140 Causewayside
Edinburgh EH9 1PR

Tel: 0131 668 2131

Liberty (formerly National Council for Civil Liberties)
21 Tabard Street
London SE1 4LA

Tel: 0171 403 3888

London Voluntary Service Council
356 Holloway Road
London N7 6PA

Tel: 0171 700 8107

National Council for Voluntary Organisations (NCVO)
Regent's Wharf
8 All Saints Street
London N1 9RL

Tel: 0171 713 6161

National Self Help Support Centre
Regent's Wharf
8 All Saints Street
London N1 9RL

Tel: 0171 713 6161

Northern Ireland Council for Voluntary Action
127 Ormeau Road
Belfast BT7 1SH

Tel: 01232 321224

Northern Ireland Volunteer Development Agency
Annsgate House
70–74 Ann Street
Belfast BT1 4EH

Tel: 01232 236100

Office of Care and Protection (Northern Ireland)
Royal Court of Justice
PO Box 410
Chichester Street
Belfast BT1 3JF

Tel: 01232 235111

Pensions Ombudsman
11 Belgrave Road
London SW1V 1RB

Tel: 0171 834 9144

Pre-Retirement Association
Nodus Centre
University of Surrey
Guildford
Surrey GU2 5RX

Tel: 01483 259747/8

(Promotes good practice. Research, information, publications)

Registrar of Companies (England and Wales)
Companies House
Crown Way
Cardiff CF4 3UZ

Tel: 01222 388588

Registrar of Companies (Northern Ireland)
IDB House
64 Chichester Street
Belfast BT1 4JX

Tel: 01232 234488

Registrar of Companies (Scotland)
100–102 George Street
Edinburgh EH2 3DJ

Tel: 0131 225 5774

Registrar of Friendly Societies
15 Great Marlborough Street
London W1V 2AX

Tel: 0171 437 9992

Scottish Council for Voluntary Organisations
18–19 Claremont Crescent
Edinburgh EH7 4QD

Tel: 0131 556 3882

Scottish Office Voluntary Sector Branch
Social Services Group
43 Jeffrey Street
Edinburgh EH1 1DG

Tel: 0131 244 5464

Shelter (National Campaign for Homeless People)
88 Old Street
London EC1V 9HU

Tel: 0171 253 0202

Shelter (Scotland)
8 Hampton Terrace
Edinburgh EH12 5JD

Tel: 0131 313 1550

Standing Conference of Voluntary Organisations (Wales)
5 Dock Chambers
Bute Street
Cardiff CF1 6AG

Tel: 01222 492 443

Terrence Higgins Trust
52–54 Gray's Inn Road
London WC1X 8JU

Tel: 0171 831 0330

(HIV/AIDS issues, advance directives)

Unemployed Voluntary Action Fund
Comely Park House
80 New Road
Dunfermline
Fife KY12 7EJ

Tel: 01383 620780

(Funding agency)

University of the Third Age (National Office)
1 Stockwell Green
London SW9 9JF

Tel: 0171 737 2541

(Forum, educational, creative, leisure)

Volunteer Centre UK
29 Lower Kings Road
Berkhamsted
Hertfordshire HP4 2AB

Tel: 01442 873311

(Information, advice, publications)

Volunteering in Wales Fund
Llys Ifor
Crescent Road
Caerphilly
Mid Glamorgan CF8 1XL

Tel: 01222 869224

(Funding agency)

Wales Council for Voluntary Action
Llys Ifor
Crescent Road
Caerphilly
Mid Glamorgan CF8 1XL

Tel: 01222 869224

INDEX

D

E

M

N

O

P

R

S

T

U

V

W